Easy Walks in Massachusetts

(second edition)

Bellingham, Blackstone, Douglas, Franklin, Grafton,
Hopedale, Medway, Mendon, Milford, Millis, Millville,
Northbridge, Upton, Uxbridge, Wrentham,
and Woonsocket RI

Marjorie Turner Hollman

Copyright © July, 2016 Marjorie Turner Hollman

MarjorieTurner.com

ISBN: 978-0-9892043-4-7

Please do not copy or distribute this copyrighted book. Copies are available on Amazon.com or from the publisher.

Maps produced using information from the U.S. Geological Survey

Digital icons open sourced from clker.com

Easy Walks in Massachusetts, second edition. Bellingham, Blackstone, Douglas, Franklin, Grafton, Hopedale, Medway, Mendon, Milford, Millis, Millville, Northbridge, Upton, Uxbridge, Wrentham, and Woonsocket, RI

1. Non-fiction 2. Sports and Recreation 3. Hiking 4. Biking 5. Family activities

6. Southern New England outdoor activities 7. Expanded 2nd edition

Disclaimer: The author and contributors to this book make no representation of accuracy of content, nor guarantee rights of access to any places described herein. Users of this book indemnify and hold harmless the author and contributors.

MarjorieTurner.com

Bellingham, MA 02019

Dedication

For my grandboys, David, Liam, and Malachi

and grandgirls, Nicole and Eowyn

Table of Contents

Key to Map Symbols 12

Bellingham **13**

    High Street Ball Fields 15

    North Maple Street Trail 19

    Silver Lake Park 23

    SNETT Bellingham 27

    Bellingham Town Common 31

    Stall Brook Trail 35

    Arcand Park 39

Blackstone **43**

    Blackstone Gorge 45

    SNETT Blackstone 49

Douglas **51**

    SNETT Douglas 53

    Douglas State Park 57

Franklin **61**

    Sculpture Park 63

    Beaver Pond (Chilson Beach) 67

    Delcarte Conservation Area 71

    SNETT Franklin 75

    Dacey Athletic Fields 79

    Indian Rock 83

Grafton 85

    Silver Lake, Grafton 87

    Gummere Woods 91

Hopedale 93

    Hopedale Parklands 95

Medway 99

    Choate Park 101

    Medway Community Farm 105

    Charles River, Sanford Mill 109

    Idylbrook 113

    Charles River, Village Street 117

Mendon 119

    Meadow Brook Woods 121

Milford 125

    Upper Charles Trail 127

Millis **131**

    Cedariver 133

    Tangerini Farm/Pleasant Meadow... 137

    Village Street Walking Path 141

    Oak Grove Farm 145

Millville **147**

    SNETT/Blackstone River Bikeway-Millville 149

Northbridge **153**

    Lookout Rock 155

    Plummer's Landing 159

Upton **163**

    CCC Camp Upton State Forest 165

    Upton State Forest Pleasant St 169

    Whitney Conservation Area 173

    Warren Brook 177

    Stefans Farm 181

Uxbridge **185**

    River Bend Farm 187

    Goat Hill 191

    Rice City Pond 195

    Cormier Woods 199

    SNETT Uxbridge 203

    Pout Pond 207

    West Hill Dam 211

Wrentham 215

    Joe's Rock 217

    Birchwold Farm 221

    Knuckup Hill 225

    Trout Pond 229

Woonsocket, RI 233

    Blackstone River Bikeway 235

Resources 239

Author's Note 241

Acknowledgments

As soon as the first edition of *Easy Walks in Massachusetts* came out, I started hearing, "Please put our town in your next edition." In response to these requests, here is the second, revised edition of the first book in what has become a series of trail guides. Several people, including Marcella Stasa, Bill Taylor, Ellen Arnold of Friends of Upton State Forest, and Al Sanborn of Grafton, have been instrumental in helping me locate as well as walk the trails of their respective towns.

I am indebted to my walking buddies as well as others I've consulted about local trails. Thanks to Mary Beauchamp, Bonnie Combs, Marc Connelly; Mary Greendale, Sandra Hayden Henry, Dale Hurd, Vickie Jaquette, Christine Keddy, Seema Kenny, Carolle Lawson, Catherine Mazurowski, Jennifer Powell, Sue and Dave Richardson, Pam Rodriques, Anna, Nicole, and David Rogers, Robert Weidknecht, and especially to my husband, Jon.

I've learned a lot about Rhode Island trails from folks I met through my Facebook page, also called *Easy Walks in Massachusetts*. Special thanks to Sue Stephenson, Joyce Chamberlain, Ben Cote, Alex Kemp, and Ernie Germani for their walking and sharing.

And my deepest gratitude for topnotch editing of this book by Francie King. Any remaining mistakes are my own.

Introduction

Most trails listed here are in the Blackstone River Valley, while a few are in towns in the Upper Charles River watershed. Some offer opportunities for kayaking and canoeing, many welcome dogs, and others accommodate horseback riding; a few also permit mountain biking. The rail-trails included here welcome walkers, runners, baby strollers, and bikes; some accommodate horses as well. A few trails in this book are handicapped accessible. Several others are newly developed. Trails only in the planning phases were not included.

Many trails listed here are relatively short—one to two miles on average—and most are well maintained. Many are wide enough to allow for families to walk together side by side. Several properties have additional connecting trails for those who are interested in longer, more challenging walks.

Location maps are provided, but these are neither trail maps nor do they accurately indicate property boundaries. I recommend downloading detailed trail maps using search terms indicated in the trail listings. My hope is that the reader will better understand how to find trailheads and will see where some are connected or quite near others. I also want to encourage walkers to visit additional trails that are nearby, sometimes right around the corner.

Trail access and trail conditions may change over time, and rights of access (parking, trail routes) cannot always be guaranteed. Avoid blocking roads, gates, or access points with cars or other vehicles. "People trails" have appeared over time and these may not honor known town or accessible properties. It's important to respect all posted and private properties.

Use common sense while outdoors. Wear comfortable, closed-toe shoes to protect your feet. Bring water, preferably in a light backpack that leaves your hands free. Hats are helpful. Windbreakers and/or raincoats can make the difference between a fun walk and a miserable one. Dress in layers.

Most hikes listed here are all relatively easy—hence the book's title! But be aware that falls, tripping hazards, slippery wet rocks, and other accidents are always possible.

Learn to recognize poison ivy, which is ubiquitous in the eastern U.S. The hairy roots of poison ivy, sometimes quite large, can climb many trees, and they are as poisonous as the plant's foliage. Winter is no protection, so do use caution. Technu and Zanfel brand topical lotions are helpful in preventing or mitigating the worst effects of this plant.

Ticks are a concern in almost any weather, but especially in spring and after a rain. Wearing light-colored clothing will help you spot these disease vectors. You can tuck your long pants into your boots or socks to discourage ticks from finding ankle skin to latch onto. "Tick checks" at the end of hikes are a good practice.

Fall is hunting season in New England. The Trustees of Reservations allows hunting on almost all of their properties, and many state parks in Massachusetts allow hunting. Mass Audubon properties *never* allow hunting. If you're uncertain about the likelihood of hunters being near trails you're on, dress both yourself and your dogs, if they're with you, in blaze orange.

Always let someone know where you are going. Cell phones often have little or no reception in the woods, especially in hilly areas, so do not depend on them for seeking help.

Try to avoid taking walks close to dusk. The sun sets quickly in winter, and a darkened, unfamiliar trail is a perfect opportunity for injury. Carry a flashlight—or better still, a headlamp—in your pack, just in case. Don't treat the outdoors as a place where "carefree" means "careless."

Most important, get outside and have fun!

Key to Map Symbols

wheelchair accessible

restrooms

horseback riding permitted

no dogs allowed

paved bicycle trail

canoe access

dogs on leash

unimproved bike trail

swimming beach

numbered road

trail

fishing

approx. property boundary

parking

surface waters

Bellingham

BELLINGHAM

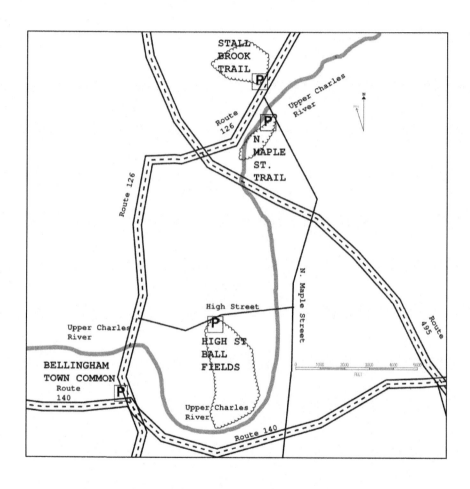

BELLINGHAM

High Street Ball Fields

Features: Secluded spot on the Upper Charles River. Side trails lead into marshland of the Charles River Meadowlands floodplain.

Trail Map: None presently available.

GPS Coordinates: 42°05'37.91"N 71°28'11.84"W

BELLINGHAM

<u>Directions</u>: From Rt. 495, take Bellingham exit 18, travel south on Rt. 126 for 1.5 miles to a blinking light, turn left onto High St., and continue 0.5 mile to ball fields on right. Or from Rt. 495 Franklin exit 17, travel north toward Bellingham on Rt. 140 about 1 mile and take a right onto N. Maple St., then travel 1 mile to High St. on the left. High St. fields are 0.5 mile on the left.

<u>Cost</u>: Free.

<u>Bathrooms</u>: Near ball fields, open during events. Also porta-potties.

<u>Best time to visit</u>: Year-round. Insect repellent needed except in late fall and winter.

<u>Trail Conditions</u>: Broad, relatively level unimproved track. Easy walking, but watch for several forks in the trail; some lead off into marshy areas. Head due south to reach the river. Trail is well marked with bright red arrows.

<u>Distance</u>: About 0.5 mile from trailhead to the banks of the Charles River.

<u>Parking</u>: Large parking area next to the ball fields.

The High Street trail is very scenic—and my favorite trail in Bellingham. There is now a prominent kiosk at the trailhead. Walk toward the ball field on the far right near the woods, near the tall black bat boxes. (Eagle Scout Sean Boddy provided this kiosk, the bridge over the intermittent stream, and trail markings.) Trail leads

BELLINGHAM

toward a substantial floodplain of the Charles River, and to the banks of the river itself. Mosquito repellent is a necessity until frost.

The path has few rocks or tree roots. Off-road vehicles have created numerous sidetracks that can be confusing, but the path is quite well marked with red arrows.

Head due south till you come to the water, which is quite shallow and about eight feet wide, at the banks of the Charles River. Look for signs of beaver across the river. The embankment is quite steep.

There is an abandoned house foundation quite near the riverbank, as well as the remnants of a dam. These stone structures, along with stone walls in the area, are all reminders of life lived near the river in years past.

BELLINGHAM

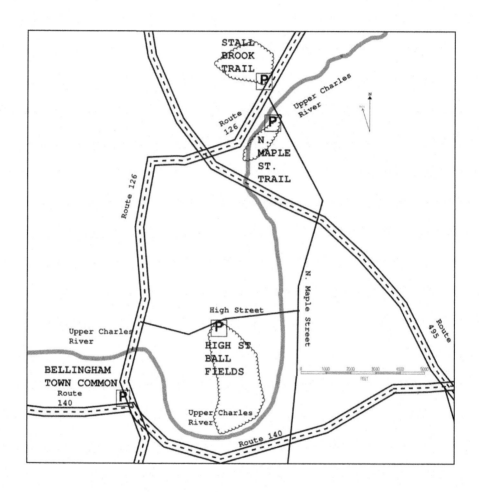

BELLINGHAM

North Maple Street Trail

Features: Small waterfall at trailhead. Access to trails along the Upper Charles River.

Trail Map: None presently available.

GPS Coordinates: 42°07'10.58"N 71°27'14.84"W

Directions: From Rt. 495 Bellingham exit 18, travel north on Rt. 126 toward Medway. Go 0.5 mile past shopping centers. At the

BELLINGHAM

next light, turn right onto N. Maple St. At 0.25 mile, turn right just before guardrail into a small pull-off next to the Charles River, across from Scandia Kitchens. Parking is not marked.

Cost: Free

Bathrooms: None available.

Best Time to Visit: Year-round, but trails are less accessible in spring because of flooding. The area is used by hunters in the fall. Use caution, wear blaze orange.

Trail Conditions: Wide, unmarked, unimproved track, trails poorly maintained, wet near trailhead in spring.

Distance: 0.5 mile, a network of trails. Avoid power plant property due south of the trailhead.

Parking: On the north side of the Charles River, you'll find a small pull-off (unmarked) for about three cars across the street from Scandia Kitchens. This is U.S. Army Corps of Engineers property. Do not block access to the dam. Walk south on N. Maple St. about 50 feet to the trailhead at the south bank of the river.

The Charles River flows past an old mill building (presently housing Scandia Kitchens) as it crosses under N. Maple St., very close to Rt. 126 in North Bellingham. There is conservation land on the south side of the river. Access has been made more difficult by the placement of large boulders next to the guardrail that is on

BELLINGHAM

N. Maple St. A sign noting "conservation land" is at the trailhead, on the south side of the river.

Small seasonal streams present a barrier to the network of trails, but the water dries up in the fall. The paths beyond the dam continue near the river.

The Charles River is still relatively small as it wends its way through Bellingham on the way to Boston. The Upper Charles River begins in Hopkinton. Several additional trails included in this book (in Milford, Medway and Millis) offer views of this sometimes-elusive river. Years ago, small waterways of this size were all potential sources of power. Clearly evident are remnants of an old dam, the property of the Army Corps of Engineers.

BELLINGHAM

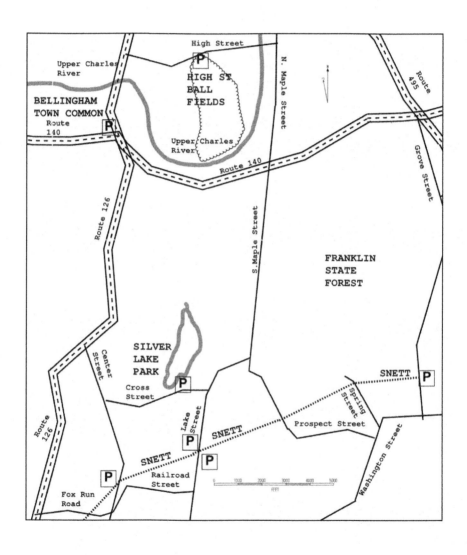

BELLINGHAM

Silver Lake Park

Features: Playground, swimming; no lifeguards, easy canoe launch, migrating waterfowl in spring and fall.

Trail Map: N/A; small open park, no real trails.

GPS Coordinates: 42°03'33.31"N 71°27'54.65"W

BELLINGHAM

Directions: From the intersection of Rts. 140 and 126 (Bellingham Center), head south 1.5 miles on Rt. 126. Turn left at Center St. (across from VFW Hall); next left (0.25 mile) is Cross St. Travel 0.5 mile on Cross St. to Silver Lake Park, on left.

Cost: Permit required for parking from Memorial Day to Labor Day. Permit is free for Bellingham residents; non-residents pay $50 for a parking permit, obtained at DPW on Blackstone St. Permit is good for both Silver Lake and Arcand Park parking.

Bathrooms: Porta-potties seasonally.

Best time to visit: Open spring, summer, fall. The park-beach area is closed in winter (December-March).

Trail conditions: While there is no trail at the playground, boaters may explore trails on the island, although paths there are overgrown.

Distance: Not applicable; this is a small open park.

Parking: Ample parking in lot next to the lake.

The playground equipment at Silver Lake offers opportunities for children to climb, swing, slide, and more. A splashpad is planned as well, but has not been installed yet.

This quiet pond offers summer swimming as well as novice-level canoeing and kayaking. No motorized boats are allowed. If you have a boat, you may want to head to the island in the middle of the lake, where small paths traverse the length of the island.

BELLINGHAM

Late July to early August is a great time for blueberrying. Because the island has become overgrown, most fruit is hanging over the water, so berry picking from a canoe or kayak is your best bet to get enough blueberries for a pancake supper! Watch for great blue herons, kingfishers, swans, mallards, occasional osprey, muskrats, and migrating waterfowl in the spring and fall.

Silver Lake is part of the Peters River, which flows directly into the Blackstone River in the adjacent town of Woonsocket, RI. The river was dammed as a source of industrial power more than 100 years ago. The dam is now maintained for recreational purposes. Earlier known as Hoag Lake, Silver Lake once boasted a hotel, a carousel, and a dance hall. Trolley cars brought city dwellers from Woonsocket, Franklin, and Milford to cool off and summer at the beach. Visitors today continue to swim in, boat on and play beside the waters of Silver Lake in the summer.

BELLINGHAM

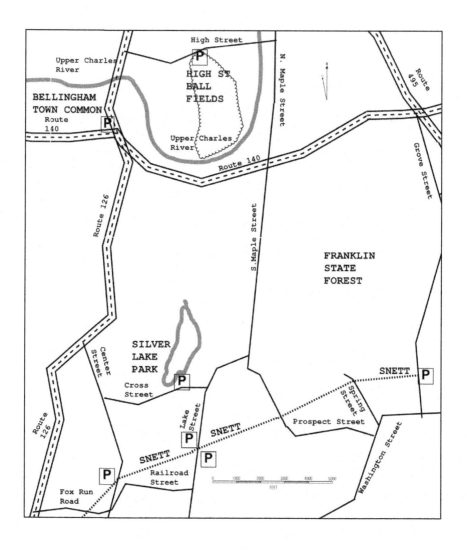

BELLINGHAM

SNETT Bellingham

Features: 0.92-mile developed portion of the partially improved 22-mile SNETT (Southern New England Trunkline Trail) rail-trail right of way. The elevated former railbed offers views of farm fields and woodlands.

Trail Map: Search online for "SNETT Trail Map."

BELLINGHAM

GPS Coordinates: 42°02'46.28"N 71°28'31.17"W (Center St.) 42°03'19.24"N 71°27'43.07"W (Lake St.)

Directions to developed section:

Center Street access: From Rt. 495 Bellingham exit 18, travel south on Rt. 126 for 2 miles to intersection of Rts. 126 and 140 (Bellingham Center). Continue south on Rt. 126 for 1 mile. Turn left at Center St. (across from VFW Hall). Just 1 mile southwest on Center St., look for SNETT kiosk, with parking signs on right, just before Fox Run Road where the trail crosses Center St.

Lake Street Access: From Rt. 495 Franklin exit 17, travel toward Bellingham on Rt. 140 North 1.3 miles to S. Maple St. (light at Charles River Bank and Rapid Refill service station). Turn left (south) onto S. Maple Street, go 1.5 miles. Turn right (west) on Lake St., at 0.6 mile park on both sides of the road where the trail crosses Lake St.

Cost: None.

Bathrooms: None.

Best time to visit: Year-round, although not maintained.

Trail conditions: The old, now-unused elevated railbed from Lake to Center St. offers level strolling on a packed stone-dust surface. It is well worth continuing onto the undeveloped portions to the east toward Franklin, as these traverse woodlands, swamps, and fields with interesting rock cuts, artifacts, and views. Swampy areas

BELLINGHAM

and motorbike-induced ruts and high humps can make walking difficult in undeveloped sections.

Distance: 0.92 miles of the 22-mile SNETT right of way.

Parking: Trail crosses and is accessed at Center St. or at Lake St.

From the Center St. kiosk, cross Center St. on the designated crosswalk to walk or bike one of the few sections of the SNETT that are complete. Gates have been installed; motorized vehicles are prohibited on this DCR-owned trail.

Near the Bellingham Sportsman's Club, the trail crosses Lake St. Use caution crossing at this point—sight lines are limited. Designated parking on Lake St. as well as crosswalks and pedestrian signs have heightened awareness, but speeding cars are a serious concern.

The trail continues toward Franklin on the other side of Lake St. Farm fields and woodlands provide most of the scenery, as well as some rock cuts and retaining walls as you approach the Franklin line. Look for the "bossy crossing" (an underpass) built at the time the railroad was constructed so the Crooks family cows could access pastureland on the other side of the tracks from where the main farm continues to operate.

Access from Rt. 126 toward Center St. is under development as part of the 2016 bridge reconstruction; however trail improvements beyond the bridge toward Center St. are planned, but not complete at this time.

BELLINGHAM

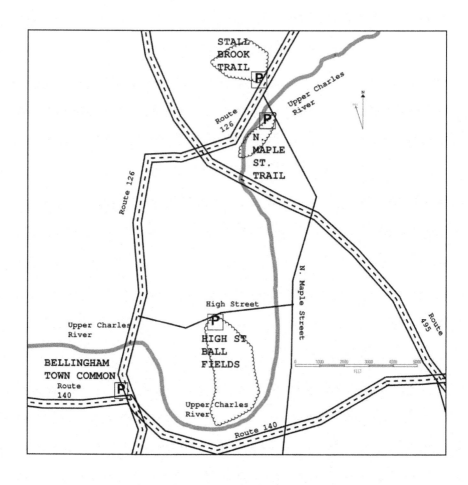

BELLINGHAM

Bellingham Town Common

Features: Playground, circular walking paths, historical markers.

Trail Map: None available.

GPS Coordinates: 42°05'16.19"N 71°28'37.41"W

Directions: From Rt. 495, Bellingham exit 18, travel south on Rt. 126 for 2 miles to intersection of Rts. 126 and 140 (Bellingham

BELLINGHAM

Center). The common is on the right, just before the intersection of Rts. 140 and 126.

Cost: None.

Bathrooms: Porta-potties in far corner next to gas station.

Best time to visit: Year-round, dawn to dusk; parking lot is not plowed in winter.

Trail conditions: Paved walkways, handicapped accessible.

Distance: A park of several acres.

Parking: Entrance to lots from Rt. 140 and Rt. 126. Room for 20 cars. Additional parking is available at shopping center across Rt. 126 (Bellingham Commons).

The Bellingham Town Common is a modern creation, constructed in 1997 on the site of an old dairy farm, more recently a grocery store. At the intersection of Rts. 140 and 126, the Bellingham Common is truly in the center of Bellingham.

A network of paved walking paths allows for easy walking loops. The small playground tucked into the back corner is away from traffic. Adequate parking is provided adjacent to the Common.

Look for granite historical markers along all the walkways, with photos of Bellingham in days gone by. Many of the photos are of the area immediately surrounding the common and reflect changes in the community. The gazebo on the common is a

BELLINGHAM

favorite spot for prom pictures, wedding photos, and multiple summer concerts. Benches offer comfortable places for parents to rest while children clamber on the playground. Dogs and skateboards are prohibited.

BELLINGHAM

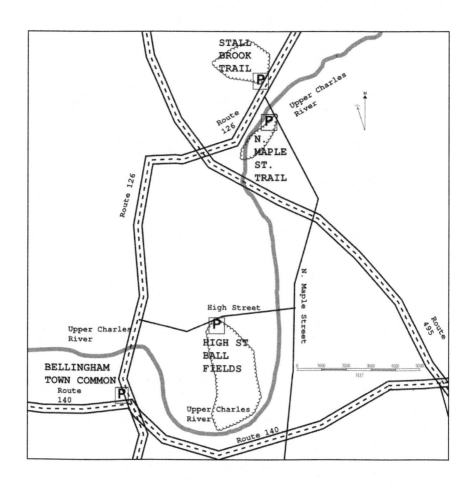

BELLINGHAM

Stall Brook Trail

Features: Rock outcroppings, pond, the Stall Brook flows past trailhead, old Army bridge provides access over the brook.

Trail Map: None presently available.

GPS Coordinates: 42°07'21.00"N 71°27'26.28"W

BELLINGHAM

<u>Directions:</u> From Rt. 495, take Bellingham exit 18, Rt. 126, head north on Rt.126 for 0.5 mile past shopping centers. Next light is Maple St. Just past the light is Stall Brook Elementary School on left.

<u>Cost:</u> None.

<u>Bathrooms:</u> None.

<u>Best Time to Visit:</u> After-school hours only; no access when school is open. After 4 p.m. weekdays during the school year.

<u>Trail Conditions:</u> Unimproved dirt track, easy, wide, unpaved trails through pine woods, some tree roots and rocks in path.

<u>Distance:</u> Network of trails, about 1 mile.

<u>Parking:</u> Only when school is not in session—after 4 p.m. on school days. Park in designated parking spaces. Trailhead is at the back of the school, on the far north side of the building. Parking as well as trail access is on school property.

An old Army surplus bridge was installed in the 1970s when teachers at Stall Brook School wanted to create a walking trail for students' use. After crossing the bridge over the Stall Brook, you can travel along the edge of the wetlands for a short distance near the brook. The path soon turns to the left, following alongside an old stone wall for much of the approximately 1 mile-long trail. The main path is wide, easy to follow, though some roots grow in the walkways.

BELLINGHAM

Alternatively, while on the main path, look for a somewhat smaller trail to the right. This will lead you to a pond and additional trails. None of these trails are marked.

BELLINGHAM

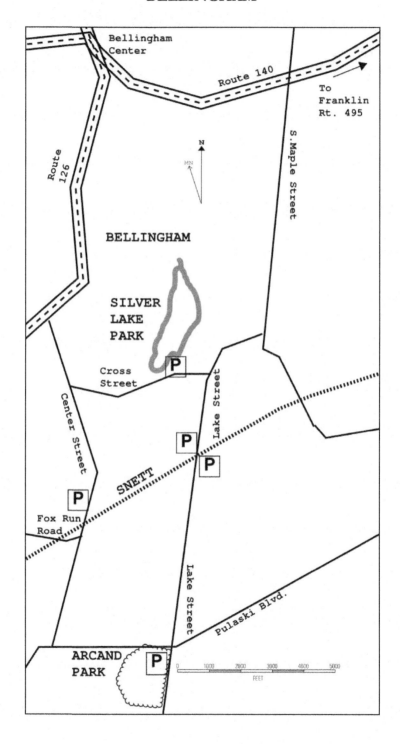

BELLINGHAM

Arcand Park

Features: Playground, boat launch at edge of pond for non-motorized boats, fishing, swimming beach, no lifeguards.

Trail Map: None presently available.

GPS Coordinates: 42°02'07.15"N 71°28'01.42"W

Directions: From intersection of Rts. 140 and 126, (Bellingham Center), travel south on Rt. 126 for 1 mile. Turn left at Center St.

BELLINGHAM

(across from VFW Hall). Travel 2 miles to intersection of Center St. and Pulaski Blvd. Turn left at light onto Pulaski, travel 0.25 mile to right at Lake St. Gated entrance to park immediately on right.

Cost: Permit is required for parking from Memorial Day to Labor Day. Permit is free for Bellingham residents, non-residents pay $50 for parking permit, obtained at Bellingham DPW (open weekdays) on Blackstone St. Permit is good for both Silver Lake and Arcand Park.

Bathrooms: Not open except for special events. Porta-potties are available in summer months.

Best Time to Visit: April-November. Park-beach area is closed in winter (December-March).

Trail Conditions: Unimproved, narrow, walkable dirt track, some varied terrain, muddy in places.

Distance: Network of trails, about 0.75 mile.

Parking: Large parking area next to pond.

Arcand Park is a town-owned recreation facility that is open seasonally. The Peters River flows south from Silver Lake through the Arcand Park property on its way south to the Blackstone River in Woonsocket, RI. Unpaved trails are on the far side of the pond, opposite the parking area and swimming beach. Swim at your own risk, as there are no lifeguards.

BELLINGHAM

Follow the shoreline around past the small dam till you find several spots where trails head off into the woods, away from the water. Watch for poison ivy, especially along the shoreline. The network of trails leading into the woods is not good for biking, but fine for walking with children, exercising dogs, or exploring in the woods. No dogs are allowed in the swimming area. Spring to fall, the gate opens at 8 a.m., and closes at 7 p.m.

This is a great place to practice paddling kayaks. Always be sure to wear flotation devices while boating. The convenient boat ramp makes this a great place for novice paddlers to start getting comfortable handling their canoes or kayaks. High bush blueberry bushes line the shores of the pond; the fruit, most easily accessed by boat, ripens in late July-early August.

Blackstone

BLACKSTONE

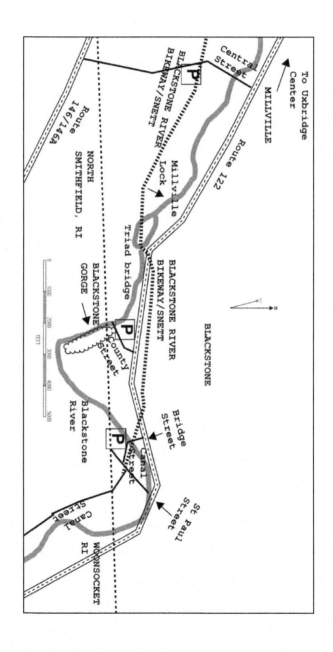

Blackstone Gorge

Features: Steep hiking trail. River views, and a boat ramp for river access just above the dam. Part of the Blackstone River Valley National Historic Park. Large quantities of mountain laurel blossoms in early summer.

BLACKSTONE

<u>Trail Map:</u> Blackstone River Valley National Historic Park trail maps available from Mass.gov website—Division of Conservation and Recreation (DCR)

<u>GPS Coordinates:</u> 42°00'55.25"N 71°33'09.33"W

<u>Directions:</u> From intersection of Rts. 16 and 122 (Uxbridge Center), take Rt. 122 south 6.75 miles, look for brown "Blackstone Gorge" sign on the right at County St., and turn right. At the end of County St. 0.3 mile, note the large parking lot on the left. The Blackstone River (which created the gorge) is directly at the end of the street.

<u>Cost:</u> None.

<u>Bathrooms:</u> None.

<u>Best Time to Visit:</u> Year-round, trail can be very icy in winter.

<u>Trail Conditions:</u> Rigorous, rocky, hilly hiking trail with some steep exposures to the river.

<u>Distance:</u> From trailhead to peak of trail, about 0.5 mile. More trails run south beyond the highest rocks along the river, but may traverse private property.

<u>Parking:</u> Large, packed dirt parking lot next to the dam and boat ramp.

While The Blackstone Gorge probably does not constitute an "Easy Walk" by my own definition, it was where I first encountered a sense of wildness in this area and is where I return, season after season, to take in the beauty of this singular place. Rocky, unmarked, well-worn paths through the Blackstone River Gorge are challenging to walk, filled with boulders and tree roots, with sections that require clambering over rocky spots that may be slippery.

The walkway slowly climbs upward, ultimately reaching 80 feet above the river. The steep cliffs of the gorge offer scenes of spectacular beauty in every season. This area near the river is filled with mountain laurel. Visit in early June to take in the large clusters of blossoms alongside the river.

Just above the dam is a quiet section of river (except in spring, when dangerous currents may make boating unsafe!) accessible by a boat ramp next to the dam. Beware of strong spring currents. The gate to the boat ramp is locked. Expect to haul a canoe or kayak about twenty yards to the water's edge.

To the north upstream is the Triad Bridge, future crossing for the SNETT/ Blackstone River Bikeway in Millville (this section of trail slated to be open fall 2016). The river is populated by numerous herons, kingfishers, osprey, and other waterfowl.

The barrels in front of the dam are sometimes dislodged by floodwaters; use care when returning to the shore, since the boat ramp is quite near the edge of the dam. A power plant water intake is just upstream. The intake current becomes quite strong close to the plant. Heed all warning signs when boating!

BLACKSTONE

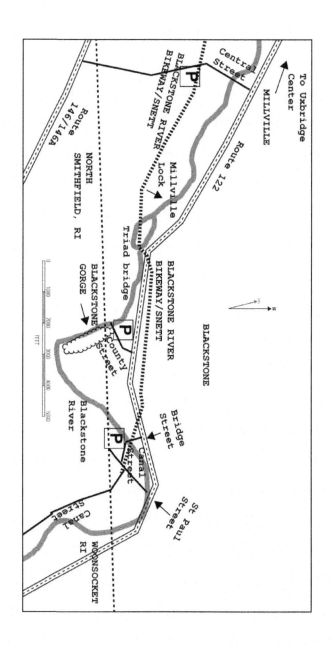

BLACKSTONE

SNETT Blackstone

Features: Paved portion of the SNETT (Southern New England Trunkline Trail) and Blackstone River Bikeway. Rock cuts, river views, part of proposed rail-trail; additional portions under development.

Trail Map: Search "SNETT Trail Map."

GPS Coordinates: 42°00'55.85"N 71°32'11.60"W

BLACKSTONE

Directions: From the intersection of Rts. 16 and 122 (Uxbridge Center), turn left to head south on Rt. 122 for 7.7 miles, through Millville into Blackstone, to a right (traffic light) at St. Paul St. At 0.3 miles, turn left onto Canal St. Travel 0.25 mile to Bridge St., large parking area on left, at corner of Canal and Bridge Sts.

Cost: None.

Bathrooms: None.

Best time to visit: Year-round, but winter access may be difficult.

Trail conditions: Paved rail-trail surface from Canal/Bridge St. to Triad Bridge, Millville.

Distance: 4 miles from Blackstone Section to Rt. 146 in Uxbridge (includes Millville section).

Parking: Large parking area just off the intersection of Bridge and Canal Sts.

This portion of the SNETT/ Blackstone River Bikeway is sure to attract national attention because of its multiple bridges over the Blackstone River. The views along the river are truly stunning: small rapids and other sections offer scenes of quiet beauty where swans and other waterfowl browse.

While great for biking or walking, don't plan on horseback riding on the Blackstone River Bikeway/SNETT in Blackstone since the surface is paved. Access is restricted until fall, 2016, when this portion should be opened to the public.

Douglas

DOUGLAS

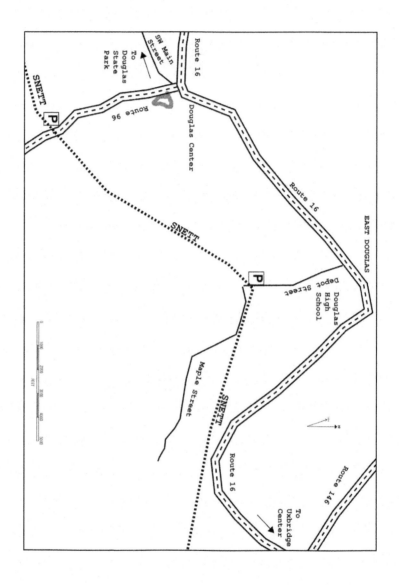

SNETT Douglas

Features: Unimproved, wide rail-trail through Douglas State Forest.

Trail Map: Search "DCR Douglas State Forest."

GPS Coordinates: (Depot Street) 42°03'41.14"N 71°42'35.52"W (South Street-Rt. 96) 42°02'49.93"N 71°44'20.11"W

DOUGLAS

<u>Directions</u>: **Behind Douglas High School:** Travel west on Rt. 16 from Rt. 146 for 3.2 miles to Depot St., turn left. Follow Depot St. 0.75 mile to parking on right.

West of Douglas Center: Travel west from Rt. 146 on Rt. 16 for 5.2 miles, Rt. 16 takes a sharp right, continue straight (not on Rt. 16) 0.1 mile to intersection with Rt. 96 just west of Douglas center. Bear left onto Rt. 96, travel 0.5 mile to parking area on the right. Trail crosses Rt. 96, trail sections are on both sides of the road. The SNETT continues through the Douglas State Forest to the Connecticut line, where the trail becomes the Airline Trail.

<u>Cost</u>: None.

<u>Bathrooms</u>: None.

<u>Best Time to Visit</u>: Year-round trail; parking area not plowed in winter.

<u>Trail Conditions</u>: Unimproved dirt rail-trail, easy, wide, unpaved.

<u>Distance</u>: 4 miles from Rt. 96 parking west to CT line; 3.5 miles from Rt. 96 east to Depot Street; 4 miles from Depot St. east to Chocolog Rd. in Uxbridge.

<u>Parking</u>: Large parking area on right, directly off Rt. 96; room for horse trailers. Parking on Depot St. behind Douglas High School.

As part of a former, continuous rail line, the SNETT in Douglas is the western terminus of the proposed 22-mile rail-trail from

DOUGLAS

Franklin to Douglas. The proposed trail continues on into Connecticut as the Airline Trail.

A popular spot for equestrians, the SNETT allows for easy access to multiple trails in this area, including the Mid-state trail as well as the Coffeehouse loop (not an easy walk!), part of the Douglas State Forest trail system.

Trail conditions do not presently lend themselves to bike riding. Loose material has been added to the trail without the necessary compaction, which makes bike riding difficult. It is fine for walking or horseback riding.

DOUGLAS

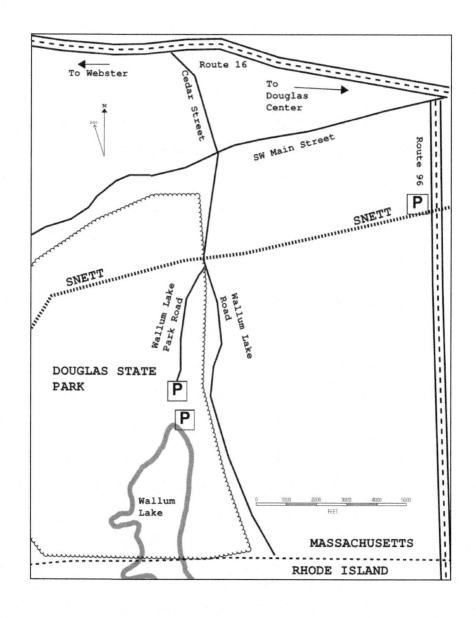

DOUGLAS

Douglas State Park

Features: Wallum Lake, boat ramp access, swimming, picnicking, multiple trails.

Trail Map: Search "DCR Douglas State Forest" then click on map.

GPS Coordinates: 42°01'26.46"N 71°46'04.66"W

Directions: West from Rt. 146 on Rt. 16 for 5.2 miles; Rt. 16 takes a sharp right. Continue straight (not on Rt. 16) for 0.1 mile to

DOUGLAS

intersection with Rt. 96 just west of Douglas center. Immediately past Rt. 96, continue on SW Main Street for 1.2 miles to left onto Wallum Lake Rd. Continue for 0.8 mile, then take right onto Wallum Lake Park Rd. Follow signs for State Park.

Cost: Fee charged during summer; free in spring, fall, and winter.

Bathrooms: At boat ramp year-round, near beach area in season.

Best Time to Visit: Year-round, though gates to major parking lots are closed after summer season.

Trail Conditions: Wide clear path to beach area, service road past nature center. Challenging rocky paths, Cedar Swamp trail interesting, but can be slippery.

Distance: Multiple trails available. Cedar Swamp trail is less than 2 miles.

Parking: Large parking areas inside the park. Parking at boat ramp is available year-round; additional parking available off-season just outside gates.

Douglas State Forest and Douglas State Park are terms that appear to be used interchangeably. The Douglas State Forest has no fee area, but the swimming area next to Wallum Lake, specifically designated as Douglas State Park, does charge a fee in the summer, and is hugely popular in warmer months, as evidenced by the hundreds of picnic tables near the waterfront of Wallum Lake.

DOUGLAS

The boat ramp into Wallum Lake allows for easy access for motorboats, as well as kayaks and canoes. This state park is quite popular with area fishermen. The swimming area has lifeguards in the summer.

Numerous trails throughout the Forest are available. The Coffee House loop is accessed from the largest parking area near the lake, but is not an Easy Walk. The Mid-State trail traverses the Douglas State Forest, crossing the path of the SNETT, but is, for the most part, not an Easy Walk.

The designated "heart-healthy" Cedar Swamp trail includes the path that travels past the Nature Center near Wallum Lake, but when approaching the cedar swamp boardwalk the trail markings are spotty. Near the nature center the trail is quite flat and offers easy walking, but we found the track down to the swamp boardwalk to be somewhat steep. The boardwalk itself can be slick in some places. The swamp offers views of downed trees from past storms, close viewing of sphagnum moss, and other swamp life. The boardwalk enables access to an otherwise impassable area.

Franklin

FRANKLIN

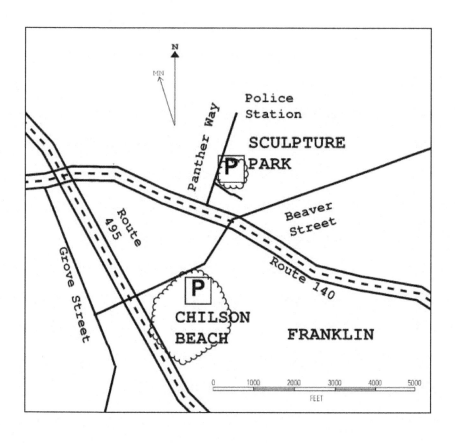

Sculpture Park

Features: Loop trail, site of former town swimming pool, rotating venue for large outdoor sculpture displays.

Trail Map: Not available.

GPS Coordinates: 42°05'24.43"N 71°24'46.62"W

FRANKLIN

<u>Directions:</u> From Rt. 495 exit 17, Franklin Rt. 140, travel toward Franklin Center on Rt. 140 past traffic light for Stop & Shop plaza. Next light (0.6 mile) is Panther Way. Turn left at light, look for the sign for Sculpture Park on the right, 0.25 mile, next to Franklin Police Station.

<u>Cost:</u> Free.

<u>Bathrooms:</u> Not available.

<u>Best Time to Visit:</u> Year-round, though the path is not plowed in winter.

<u>Trail Conditions:</u> Paved, handicapped-accessible loop trail.

<u>Distance:</u> 0.1 mile.

<u>Parking:</u> Handicapped parking accessed from Edwards St., street parking on Panther Way, and additional parking in Franklin Police Station visitor lot.

The Franklin Sculpture Park is a very new creation, constructed in 2014 on the site of the former town swimming pool. The area, actually a dammed stream, featured cement walls at each end of the pool. Abandoned in the 1970s, the pool area was filled in. Trees grew up, providing habitat for birds, frogs, turtles, chipmunks, and other wildlife. Watch for green herons that roost among the trees in the middle of the former pool area.

The town, in partnership with the Franklin Center for the Arts, constructed a handicapped-accessible loop trail using the cement walls of the former pool as part of the trail structure. A great outdoor space, it provides local artists and school children with an area where they can exhibit their sculptures on a rotating schedule. It's a great walk for any age in any season. The loop meanders through areas of full sun as well as shade in portions of the trail that are tucked into the woodland that surrounds the park.

FRANKLIN

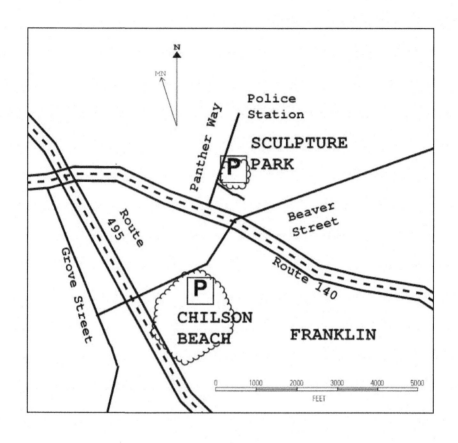

Beaver Pond (Chilson Beach)

Features: Well-worn dirt track, signs of beaver, migrating waterfowl. Swimming permitted for Franklin residents only.

Trail Map: Not presently available.

GPS Coordinates: 42°04'57.39"N 71°25'05.38"W

FRANKLIN

<u>Directions:</u> From Rt. 495 exit 17, Franklin Rt. 140, travel toward Franklin Center on Rt. 140 for 0.75 mile. At the stoplight, turn right onto Beaver St. just past Akin-Bak Farm. Beaver Pond is 0.5 mile down on left, just before the Rt. 495 overpass.

<u>Cost:</u> Free Memorial Day to Labor Day, for Franklin residents only. No beach pass required, but attendants will check for residency.

<u>Bathrooms:</u> Available in summer only.

<u>Best Time to Visit:</u> For Franklin residents only during the summer for swimming and boating. Year-round for hiking. No residence restrictions before Memorial Day and after Labor Day.

<u>Trail Conditions:</u> Unimproved, wide dirt track.

<u>Distance:</u> 0.25 mile trail alongside the eastern shore of the pond.

<u>Parking:</u> Large paved lot next to the beach area.

The sounds of Rt. 495 are inescapable, but Beaver Pond still offers a nice spot for an easy walk, with plenty of parking. Also called Chilson Beach, the pond area posts lifeguards in the summer, and offers swimming, and ballplaying in the fields.

Beyond the beach area on the left (the east side of the pond, away from Rt. 495) a trail runs along the edge of the pond. The trail bisects Beaver Pond. A marsh area, on the other side of the trail, is also fun to explore. Opportunities for birding await. The

FRANKLIN

path dead-ends at a water department access road; no public access is permitted via this road.

About three-fourths of the way to the end of the trail, another path branches off to the left, following the edges of the marsh. Look for multiple signs of beaver (happily appropriate for a recreation area on Beaver St.!). Parts of this area are somewhat obstructed by beaver activity, but still fun to explore with children, who may discover the telltale signs of the beavers' presence.

FRANKLIN

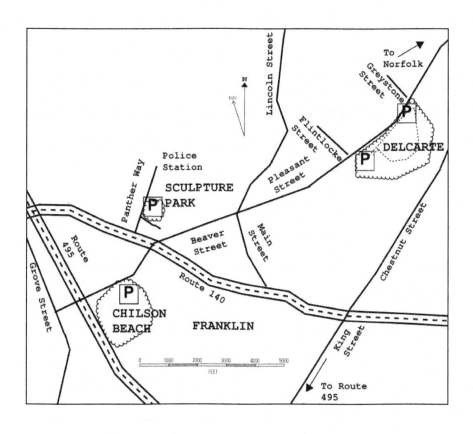

Delcarte Conservation Area

Features: Water views, catch-and-release fishing, floating bridge, loop trail, playground, picnic tables.

Trail Maps: At trailhead kiosk and throughout the trail system.

FRANKLIN

GPS Coordinates: (Across from Greystone) 42°05'52.84"N 71°22'51.84"W (Across from Flintlocke) 42°05'39.44"N 71°23'09.48"W

Directions: From Franklin's town common, take Pleasant St. toward Norfolk about 0.75 mile. Two entrances: first, an unpaved entrance on the right opposite Flintlocke Rd.; second, from a larger, paved parking area, 0.5 mile farther on right, opposite Greystone Rd. Del Carte Conservation Area signs at parking lots.

Cost: None.

Bathrooms: Porta-potties, summer only.

Best Time to Visit: Year-round.

Trail Conditions: Unimproved, wide dirt track.

Distance: 1-mile loop trail around pond with additional loops available.

Parking: Large paved lot with playground area across from Greystone Rd. Much smaller, unpaved lot near Flintlocke Rd.

This 136-acre property is managed by the Franklin Conservation Commission. Several dams, recently restored, form the ponds on the property.

The few rolling sections of trail are easily traversable. Wood chips and a small bridge over a tiny stream make for dry paths with solid footing. A section of trail near the floating bridge is rather steep. Look for trail markings to guide you to the floating bridge and away from these steepest sections near the backside of the pond. The commuter train line forms the outer boundary at the back of the property. Stay off the train tracks! The floating bridge on the far side of the pond facilitates the 1-mile loop trail. Additional trails follow the shore of a second pond on the property, to the southwest of the main pond and loop trail.

The playground adjacent to the large parking area is a whimsical structure, but has been plagued with structural problems. It has recently been repaired, and we hope any problems have been resolved.

A small boat ramp for canoes and kayaks, near the parking area across from Greystone Rd., makes entry into the pond easy. Fishing is catch-and-release only.

FRANKLIN

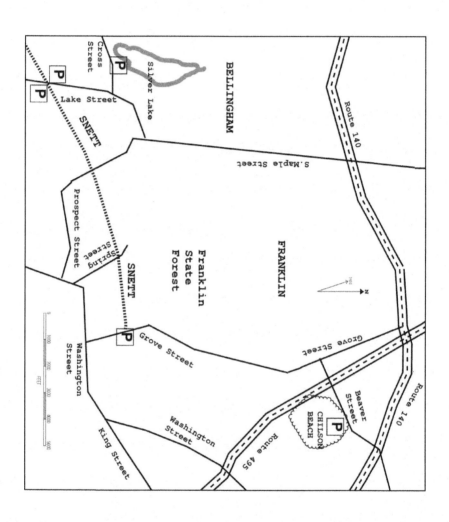

SNETT Franklin

Features: Eastern-most trailhead for 22-mile SNETT right-of-way. Stone retaining walls, steep slopes to woods below, small, scenic woodland streams.

Trail Map: Search "SNETT Trail Map."

GPS Coordinates: 42°03'43.06"N 71°25'42.55"W

Directions: **From the north:** Rt. 495 exit 17, Rt. 140, Franklin, head north toward Bellingham. Grove St. is immediately past the

FRANKLIN

interchange, so just turn left at the light. Follow Grove St. for 2 miles, look for SNETT signs. Parking is on left, trailhead on the right.

From the south: Rt. 495 exit 16, King St., head south on King St. for 0.8 mile; King St. becomes Washington St. Continue on Washington St. for another 0.5 mile to a right onto Grove St. Travel 0.5 mile. SNETT trailhead is on the left, parking is on the right.

Cost: None.

Bathrooms: None.

Best Time to Visit: Year-round..

Trail Conditions: Wide, flat, unimproved former railbed. Steep climb up and over Prospect St. where trail is obstructed. Moguls created by dirt bikes. Graded from Grove St. to Spring St.

Distance: About 1.5 miles from Grove St. to Bellingham line.

Parking: Lot for 5-7 cars across the street from Grove St. entrance. Look for signs.

This mostly unimproved former railbed/right-of-way is owned by DCR, extending from Franklin through Bellingham, Blackstone, Millville, Uxbridge, and into Douglas. The Franklin section of the Southern New England Trunkline Trail (SNETT) rail-trail is mostly graded, cleared, and still being developed. Poor drainage due to removal of the original rail ballast, as well as "humps"

FRANKLIN

caused by prohibited off-track vehicles pose both minor and major challenges in various sections.

This easternmost section in Franklin is graded but is otherwise unimproved. Proceeding west, the path crosses through the Franklin State Forest on its way to Spring St. to open farmland after 0.5 mile. Watch for poison ivy. Several trails from the Franklin State Forest intersect the SNETT, and are mostly rough, rocky, and eroded by dirt bikes. At about the 0.75-mile mark the way is blocked by a 20-foot high infill where Prospect St. intersects the trail. Crossing over Prospect St. is possible but make sure to stay off adjacent residential private properties.

From Prospect St., a 0.5-mile unimproved but passable stretch continues to the Lake St., Bellingham, parking area. This section of the path offers 20-foot-high rock cuts with original drill marks. The boundary between the Bellingham and Franklin sections is unmarked. Look for the "bossy crossing"—a former cow pasture underpass built of mortared stone—as you approach the Lake Street crossing.

The Franklin/Bellingham Rail-trail Committee sponsors events throughout the year. This group, along with others, is working to heighten public awareness of the SNETT. Check out their Facebook page for trail updates.

FRANKLIN

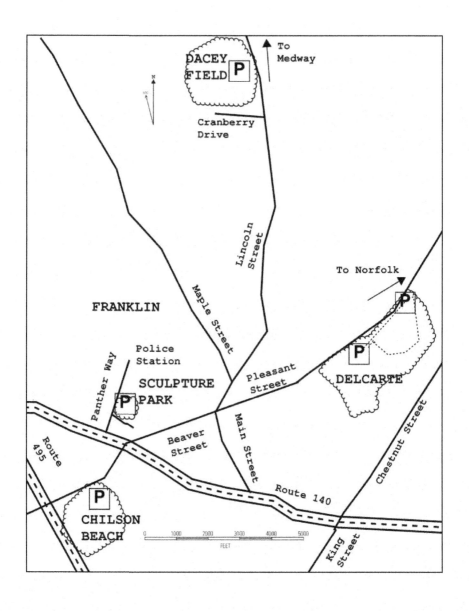

FRANKLIN

Dacey Athletic Fields

Features: Shepard's Brook, board walks, 18-hole disc-golf course.

Trail Map: Not presently available.

GPS Coordinates: 42°07'10.77"N 71°23'49.04"W

Directions: At Franklin's town common, Main St. is to the right of St. Mary's Church. Take Main St. north, away from the downtown,

FRANKLIN

0.2 mile, bear right at the little red schoolhouse, where the road becomes Lincoln St. Travel 1.5 miles, past elementary and middle schools on left. Dacey Athletic Fields are the next left, another 0.5 mile past the school complex. Trailhead is just to the left of the fenced-in dog park area. Look for a sign for Dacey Disc Golf Course.

Cost: None.

Bathrooms: Porta-potties at field near parking lot.

Best Time to Visit: Accessible year-round. Very wet in spring.

Trail Conditions: Narrow boardwalks, wide, unimproved trails, roots, rocks in trail, relatively flat.

Distance: A network of trails makes distance variable and good for short walks of under a mile, plus additional trails when following disc-golf course.

Parking: Large paved parking areas for athletic events. May be crowded depending on athletic activities.

Shepard's Brook flows through this area, headed to the nearby Charles River, which forms the boundary between Franklin and Medway. The town has built several bridges to help visitors get from one side of this picturesque brook to the other. In spring the water flows very swiftly here, but is smaller and calmer in warmer months.

FRANKLIN

The woodland trails behind the sports fields have been developed as an 18-hole disc-golf course—think "little plastic disc Frisbees." This network of trails now has arrows indicating where the "golf course" trail goes.

A separate Nature Trail is under construction. The new trail traverses some very marshy ground, with boardwalks to assist walkers through the wet areas. (We found no actual loop trail, so we eventually turned back rather than continue walking through poorly marked areas.) The disc-golf area offered more scenic views than the "Nature Trail." If you choose to walk these "golf" course trails be sure to be courteous of those using the disc-golf course.

A dog park has recently been added to the Dacey Athletic Fields complex. Dogs are permitted at the dog park; owners must leash dogs when using the trails. No dogs are allowed on the athletic fields.

The Recreation Department has posted multiple warnings on its website against sledding at the Dacey field complex. Insect repellent is advisable in warmer weather.

FRANKLIN

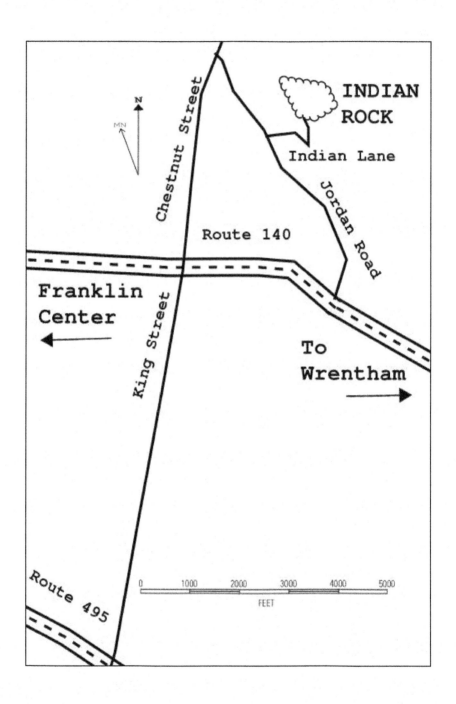

FRANKLIN

Indian Rock

Features: Large rock outcropping. Trails are not maintained.

Trail Map: Not presently available.

GPS Coordinates: 42°05'15.67"N 71°22'10.31"W

Directions: From downtown Franklin center, travel east on Rt. 140 (E. Central St.) for 0.5 mile, turn left at light onto Chestnut St., go

FRANKLIN

0.75 mile to Jordan Rd. on the right. About 0.25 mile along Jordan Rd., turn left onto Indian Lane. Take the first left onto King Philip Rd., a dead-end, and park at the end of road. Look left for a small conservation marker on a tree, opening onto the trail.

Cost: None.

Bathrooms: None.

Best Time to Visit: Year-round. Bring insect repellent in summer.

Trail Conditions: Unimproved, dirt track, fallen trees impede trails. 20-foot drop at edge of rock.

Distance: 0.25 mile to Indian Rock, and small network of unmarked trails.

Parking: Access is at the end of a dead-end street. No designated parking is provided. Avoid blocking neighbors' driveways.

Indian Rock is worth visiting for the fun of clambering on the large rock outcropping that is quite near the trailhead. No trail kiosk marks the trailhead, look for a "Franklin Conservation Commission" marker, visible on a tree near the street, where the trail heads into the woods. A few yards into the woods the path toward Indian Rock is on the right. Follow the well-worn track to the rocky outcrop. The oak-hemlock forest blocks the view. A smaller obstructed path leads to the base of the rock. Local legends connect this location with events during King Philip's war—thus the name, Indian Rock.

Grafton

GRAFTON

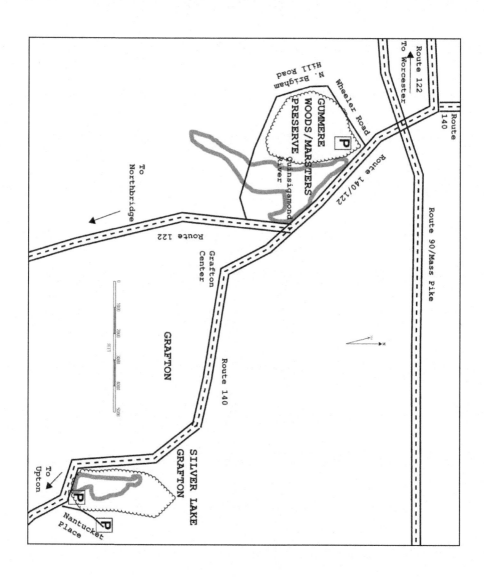

GRAFTON

Silver Lake, Grafton

Features: Town beach, swimming, trails.

Trail Map: Search "Fletcher Reserve Grafton."

GPS Coordinates: (Beach area) 42°11'23.77"N 71°39'15.84"W (Nantucket Road) 42°11'28.10"N 71°39'10.02"W

Directions: **From Grafton Center:** travel south on Rt. 140 for 2.2 miles to Silver Lake Beach on the left.

GRAFTON

From Upton: From Hartford Ave. in Upton, follow Rt. 140 north for 2.2 miles to Silver Lake beach on the right. When the beach area is closed, trails can be accessed from Nantucket Place., just south of the park, off Rt. 140.

Cost: Beach permit is required for the summer season, but access to the trails from Nantucket St. is free.

Bathrooms: Porta-potties seasonally.

Best Time to Visit: Year-round.

Trail Conditions: Clear, unimproved dirt track, marked trails, a few rocks and tree roots, relatively level.

Distance: 0.5 mile of trails.

Parking: Allowed at the beach area during summer with a permit, or on-street parking on Nantucket St. for access to trails.

Silver Lake in Grafton is a busy swimming place in summer, but very quiet in the winter. The parking gate is closed off-season, but by gaining access from Nantucket Street you can walk the trails and take in water views of this scenic spot year-round.

Beyond the beach the track becomes quite wet in a few places. The trails are unmarked but provide easy, unobstructed walking, with only a few stones in the path and the rewards may be great! Look for beavers that have built a large lodge against the shoreline. We spotted many signs of beaver throughout this area.

GRAFTON

There are large boulders at the end of the trail. The Fletcher Reserve is just north of the Silver Lake recreation area, a much rougher area. For easy walking, stick to trails near the shore adjacent to the swimming beach. The map for the Fletcher Reserve will guide you from the parking area on Nantucket Place to the backside of the Silver Lake Recreation area.

GRAFTON

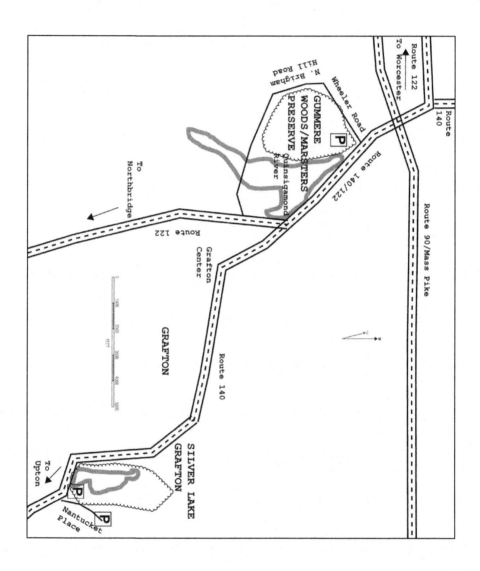

GRAFTON

Gummere Woods

Features: Water views, easy walking footpaths, boat ramp adjacent to trailhead.

Trail Map: Search "Gummere Woods Grafton."

GPS Coordinates: 42°13'16.14"N 71°42'09.84"W

GRAFTON

Directions: 11 Wheeler Rd. Near Rts. 122/140. From Grafton Center on Rt. 140, travel north 0.5 mile to intersection at Rt. 122. Continue on Rt. 140/122 another 0.75 mile to Wheeler Rd. on the left. Parking is immediately on the left on Wheeler Rd.

Cost: None.

Bathrooms: None.

Best Time to Visit: Year-round.

Trail Conditions: Clear, unimproved dirt track, marked trails, a few rocks and roots, some level trails, additional small inclines.

Distance: 1 mile of trails.

Parking: Paved parking for about 5 cars is directly off Rt. 122. There is also a boat ramp and parking area directly on Rt. 122 just southeast of Wheeler Rd.

Gummere Woods and Marsters Preserve offers water views of the Quinsigamond River, which flows past these two adjacent conservation parcels, 85 acres in total. A popular dog-walking spot.

You'll find numerous trails to choose from. Some follow right along the shoreline of the river while others head up into the woods that make up the rest of the property. The terrain offers some rolling hills and a few steeper climbs as you explore farther back away from the river.

Hopedale

HOPEDALE

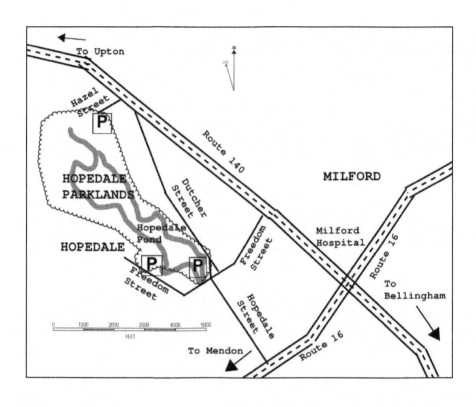

Hopedale Parklands

Features: Carriage path, water views, large boulders, boat ramp at main entrance (Dutcher/Hopedale St.). Summer swimming, lifeguards posted.

Trail Map: Not presently available.

HOPEDALE

GPS Coordinates: 42°08'03.76"N 71°32'39.36"W (main entrance on Hopedale street) 42°08'04.83"N 71°33'02.03"W (Freedom St. entrance) 42°08'53.40"N 71°33'26.50"W (Hazel St.)

Directions: Three entrances: 162 Dutcher St. (intersection with Hopedale St.); Hazel St.; and Freedom St. Details at end of section.

Cost: None.

Bathrooms: Available in summer only, near beach area at Dutcher/Hopedale Sts.

Best Time to Visit: Year-round.

Trail Conditions: Wide, well-marked, graded, unpaved carriage path, some rocks and tree roots.

Distance: About 2.25 miles to circle pond, but requires travel on the street to complete a loop.

Parking: On-street parking on Hopedale St. at main entrance; small (four cars) parking area on Freedom St., off-street parking for several cars along Hazel St.

Hopedale Parklands, or "The Parklands," as it's locally known, is at 162 Dutcher St. in Hopedale, offering over 2 miles of walking trails on 273 acres, which surround Hopedale Pond. The broad open pathways give one the sense of walking on the carriage trails of Acadia National Park (without the long drive to get there, and without the mountain views of Acadia, of course!).

HOPEDALE

The main entrance, where the town swimming beach is located, is at the intersection of Dutcher and Hopedale Sts., accessed directly from Rt. 16.

Each entrance has a different feeling. The main entrance is the most heavily used. The Hazel St. entrance is the most remote, requiring a quarter-mile walk through woodlands to reach the pond. The Freedom St. entrance is less frequently used than the entrance at Dutcher/Hopedale Sts. and has some ups and downs, but it follows the shoreline closely.

Broad trails offer lots of room for children to explore. Picnic tables and benches are available on the Dutcher/Hopedale Sts. side of the Parklands. The Mill River flows into the pond under a stone bridge. The bridge is at about the half-way mark from either the Freedom St. or Dutcher/Hopedale Sts. entrances.

The wide walkway circumnavigating the pond is mostly a gravel path. Private property along the shore of the pond near the Draper Mill prevents a complete circumnavigation of the pond by footpath.

Dutcher/Hopedale Sts. entrance: From Rt. 140 northbound, in Milford, at the Milford Regional Medical Center, turn left onto Rt. 16 westbound, continue 0.5 mile to the next light, turn right onto Hopedale St. Drive past the Draper Mill complex to the intersection with Freedom St (0.5 mile). Continue straight on Hopedale St. The pond is ahead on the left. Street parking is

HOPEDALE

straight ahead and is permitted on both sides of Hopedale St. up to Dutcher St., the actual address for the park.

Freedom St. entrance: Follow directions above to intersection of Hopedale and Freedom St. Turn left onto Freedom St., drive past Draper Mill. Freedom St. bears sharply right almost immediately past the mill. Just past a small neighborhood, 0.5 mile from the intersection of Freedom and Hopedale Streets, a gated entrance to the Parklands is on the right with space for four cars.

Hazel St. entrance: Hazel St. is a short, dead-end road accessed from Rt. 140. From the intersection of Rts. 140 and 16 at Milford Hospital, continue north toward Upton on Rt. 140 almost 2 miles. Hazel St. is on the left, quite near Whitcomb House on the right. Near the end of Hazel St., 0.1 mile, is a yellow park gate and kiosk, with parking for several cars. Do not block the gate. Walk about 0.25 mile to the pond from parking on Hazel St.

Medway

MEDWAY

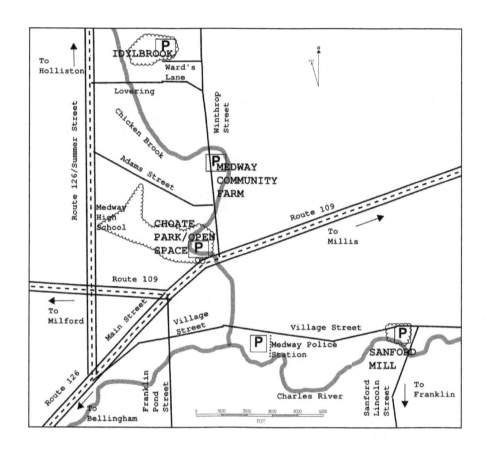

MEDWAY

Choate Park

Features: Stone walls along a woodland path from pond to Medway High School, a circular trail around the pond, and a waterfall at the entrance to the park. This is the beginning of a proposed "Link Trail" to Holliston.

Trail Map: Search: "Medway MA open space" (then click on "Brochure") to download very basic map.

MEDWAY

GPS Coordinates: 42°08'52.98"N 71°25'38.69"W

Directions: From the intersection of Main St. and Rt. 109 in Medway (Medway Community Church), head northeast 0.2 mile on Rt. 109 toward business district. Turn left onto Mechanic St., then quickly turn right at Oak St. Follow the road past the Thayer House; parking is adjacent to the park area.

Cost: None.

Bathrooms: Porta-potties next to the ball fields adjacent to the park.

Best Time to Visit: Year-round, and parking lot is plowed in winter.

Trail Conditions: Wide, dirt track, graded around pond, level, unimproved track between pond and Medway High School.

Distance: The path around the pond is a little over 0.25 mile; the path between the park and Medway High School is a little over 0.5 mile. An additional 0.25-mile section of trail has recently been constructed behind the high school through woods, almost out to Adams Street. Not a loop trail.

Parking: Large paved parking area next to Choate Pond. Additional parking is at the end of the trail in back of Medway High School near Adams St.; parking is permitted when school is not in session.

A fifteen-foot waterfall (part of Chicken Brook) cascades over the dam that created Choate Pond, right next to the parking area. The

MEDWAY

pond is open for swimming in summer, but there are no lifeguards. High bacteria counts can close the pond for swimming.

The walking path encircling Choate Pond is a rolling, graded track. The trailhead, on the far side of Choate Pond, has a "Medway Open Space" blue sign; it's level, with few tree roots, and leads directly to Medway High School.

The Medway Open Space committee has recently completed an additional trail link that wends through woods behind Medway High School, out to an open field that borders Adams St., then up to a parking area at the back of the school. Nicely planned, the entire trail system offers easy walking for young and old alike.

An additional "Link Trail" is planned to connect from near Adams St., northward toward Lovering St. The plan is to link the area from Medway High School north to Lovering St., then to create an additional link to Idylbrook sports fields and conservation area (See Idylbrook, Medway section, in *Easy Walks*).

MEDWAY

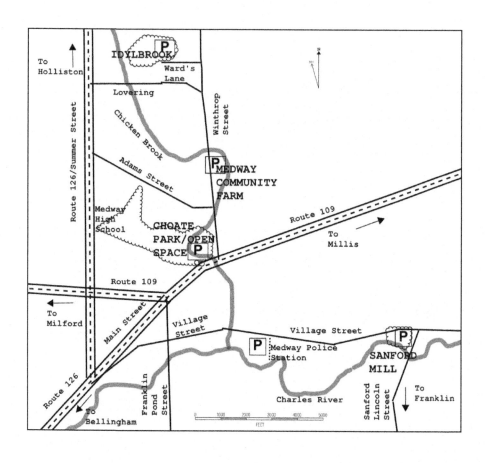

MEDWAY

Medway Community Farm

Features: Views of Chicken Brook, self-guided trail, open farm fields, CSAs, farm stand in summer.

Trail Map: Search "Medway MA Open Space" then click on Medway Community Farm map.

GPS Coordinates: 42°09'30.68"N 71°25'38.85"W

MEDWAY

Directions: From intersection of Rt. 109 and Main St. in Medway, (Medway Community Church), travel 0.5 mile to left onto Winthrop St., then continue north 0.75 mile. The farm is on the right (look for the Medway Community Farm sign).

Cost: Free.

Bathrooms: No.

Best Time to Visit: Year-round.

Trail Conditions: Mostly level, marked, self-guided trail.

Distance: 0.5 mile loop trail.

Parking: Hard-packed gravel parking area at farm stand.

The Medway Community Farm teamed with the Medway Open Space Committee to create a new self-guided trail system. The trail utilizes edges of the community farm as well as a parcel of adjacent Medway open space to provide an interactive trail experience for farm visitors. Interpretive signs explain important features of the farm.

Take in sweeping views of this organic community farm as you walk the trail. Chicken Brook can best be seen in the late fall, winter, and early spring before shrubs have leafed out. The brook borders one side of the farm.

A hands-on camp for children is offered each summer at the farm. Registration is handled by the Medway Community Education department.

MEDWAY

Be sure to stop by the honor-system farm stand during the summer season to get farm-fresh produce, and then head out onto the trail while you're visiting. The farm also offers CSA (Community Supported Agriculture) shares in season.

MEDWAY

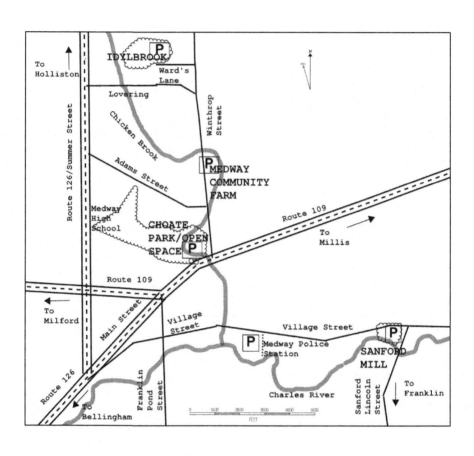

MEDWAY

Charles River, Sanford Mill

Features: Loop trail, boat launch into Upper Charles River, large flat rock in river, favorite sunning place for swimmers in years gone by.

Trail Map: Search for "Medway MA Open space" then click on "Brochure."

GPS Coordinates: 42°08'21.45"N 71°23'53.97"W

MEDWAY

Directions: Take Village St. in Medway to Medway Town Hall; Sanford St (Lincoln Street in Franklin). is adjacent to the town hall. Turn right onto Sanford St. Sanford Mill Condo Complex is on the right, just behind the town hall. Turn into the driveway, stay to the right, and proceed to the back of the buildings. Look for the trailhead sign off the pavement, toward the river.

Cost: None.

Bathrooms: None.

Best Time to Visit: Year-round.

Trail Conditions: Wide, unimproved dirt track, well marked.

Distance: About 50 yards to the river. The trail follows a loop in an area formerly known as the "Amphitheater." The loop is about 0.25 mile in length.

Parking: At the back of a condo development, a circular dirt driveway off the edge of the pavement allows for parking for 3-4 cars.

The only public access to the Charles River in this area is through a private condominium complex, the Sanford Mill. Park only in designated trail parking spots to make sure other cars are not blocked. Although access is by way of private property, a legal easement ensures public access to this conservation property with frontage on the Charles River.

MEDWAY

Directly behind the Medway Town Hall on Village St., this area was once the town picnic spot, known as "The Amphitheater." Thanks to the efforts of local volunteers, the Medway Conservation Commission, and Medway Open Space members, invasive plants that once choked the four-acre parcel have been removed.

A loop trail as well as a small boat ramp is available to provide access to the Charles River. The "Medway Open Space" sign directs walkers to the circular trail that heads down to the river, along the shore a short distance, and then loops back to the beginning of the trailhead.

MEDWAY

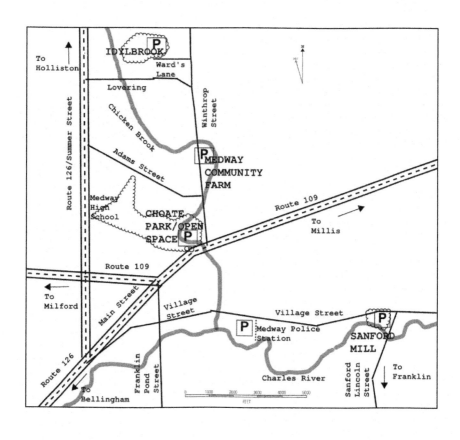

Idylbrook

Features: Vernal pools in woods, stone walls, views of Chicken Brook.

Trail Map: Search "Medway Open Space" then click on Idylbrook maps.

GPS Coordinates: 42°10'10.09"N 71°26'04.25"W

MEDWAY

Directions: From the intersection of Rt. 109 and Main St. in Medway (Medway Community Church), travel 0.5 mile east to Winthrop St. Turn left onto Winthrop St., then travel 1.5 miles to Partridge St. Turn left onto Partridge St., continue straight onto Ward's Lane, and follow signs to Idylbrook Fields, about 0.3 mile. There are two trailheads: one to the left as you park, and the other to the far right of the athletic fields.

Cost: None.

Bathrooms: Porta-potties seasonally at the edge of the fields.

Best Time to Visit: Year-round.

Trail Conditions: Wide, unimproved dirt track, some muddy spots.

Distance: A network of trails, 0.5 mile long, with numerous additional trails leading into Holliston through the easement over private land.

Parking: Large gravel parking areas next to soccer fields, accessed from Ward's Lane or Kimberly Dr.

Idylbrook has a large athletic field with substantial parking. Two trailheads are available. Access from Kimberly Dr. parking leads to a network of trails, vernal pools, and small seasonal streams that flow through the area. Trails are open, relatively flat, and easily navigable.

MEDWAY

The second trail, accessed from Ward's Lane, leads directly to a beaver pond, actually part of Chicken Brook, which then flows south into Choate Pond.

Loop around to the right to connect with the path that begins on the opposite side of the athletic fields. Additional paths cross private property (Betania II Marian Retreat Center) offering opportunities for much longer walks that connect with Wenakeening Woods in Holliston, as well as the Upper Charles Trail in Holliston. Permission to travel across Betania's private property is conditional upon walkers keeping dogs on leashes at all times.

MEDWAY

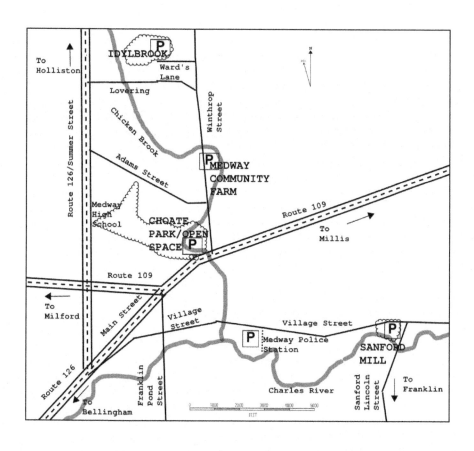

Charles River, Village Street

Features: Benches, access to Upper Charles River.

Trail Map: Search: "Medway MA Open space" then click on "Brochure" to download very basic map.

GPS Coordinates: 42°8'24.68"N 71°25'31.30"W

MEDWAY

Directions: Next to Medway Police Station, 315 Village St.

Cost: None.

Bathrooms: No.

Best Time to Visit: Year-round.

Trail Conditions: Wide, graveled path.

Distance: 20 yards.

Parking: Visitor parking at the Medway Police Station.

A quick walk brings you to a view of the Charles River on this very short trail. A memorial to Medway Boy Scout leader, Kurt Ohnemus, the trail and benches were built by his son as an Eagle Scout project. Several stone benches sit at the river's edge.

Parking is available at the Police Station, 315 Village St. Park only in designated parking spots. Facing the station, look to the left for the opening, which is to the left of the parking lot, close to the street. It is only a short walk to the river, as the path threads its way between the Police Station parking and the adjacent house. But it is indeed a trail, a quiet memorial, and the public is welcome to respectfully visit.

Mendon

MENDON

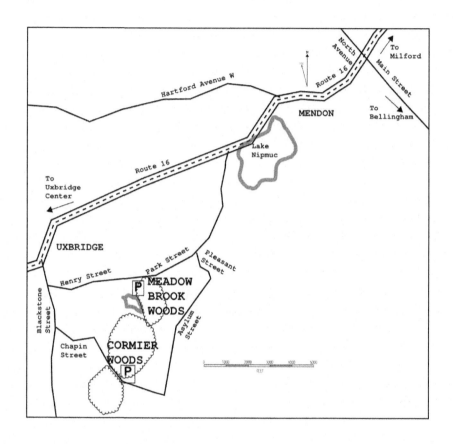

MENDON

Meadow Brook Woods

Features: Woodland trail to bridges crossing Meadow Brook, trail connects with Cormier Woods in Uxbridge.

Trail Map: Search "Cormier Woods" then click on Trustees of Reservations website "Maps & Resources," then download map for Cormier Woods/Meadow Brook Woods.

GPS Coordinates: 42°04'53.23"N 71°35'25.14"W

MENDON

Directions: Take Rt. 16 west from Mendon Center (Main St. and North Ave.) 3.3 miles. Turn left onto Blackstone St. (at island with Uxbridge sign). Travel 0.2 mile to Henry St. on the left, and turn left. Henry becomes Park St. in Mendon (about 0.75 mile). Trail is on the right where the road becomes Park St.

Cost: None.

Bathrooms: None.

Best Time to Visit: Year-round.

Trail Conditions: Wide unimproved dirt track, some muddy spots, two bridges over streams, rough, rocky in some spots.

Distance: About 1+ miles of trail connecting with multiple additional trails at Cormier Woods, Uxbridge.

Parking: Pull-off area along the road on Park St. for two cars next to the sign for Meadow Brook Woods. Some parking is also available on the opposite side of the street.

Meadow Brook Woods is initially quite hilly, but becomes mostly level once you walk a short distance. Trail markings begin right near the Meadow Brook Woods sign near the road, continue up a rather steep hill, then onto trails that are on a gentler incline.

The marked trail eventually leads across two bridges to meet up with the trail to Cormier Woods (marked on the Trustees map of Cormier Woods and Meadow Brook Woods as the white trail) in Uxbridge (see Uxbridge section of *Easy Walks*).

MENDON

The bridges over the two small streams that flow through this woodland area offer some pretty views. Ledge in this area can make for some challenging footing.

For longer and more challenging trails, continue on to Cormier Woods. Access to the Mendon Town Forest from this area is possible, but the Town Forest is very poorly marked and quite popular with hunters.

The Trustees of Reservations allows hunting on many of their properties, including this area. Blaze orange clothing is a *must* in the fall, winter, and early springtime.

Milford

MILFORD

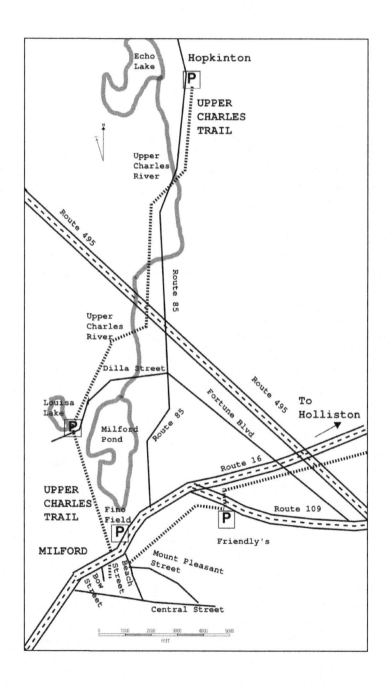

MILFORD

Upper Charles Trail

Features: Louisa Lake, paved bicycle-walking rail-trail, very popular. Continuous trail from Hopkinton town line through downtown Milford, then up to Holliston Center.

Trail Map: Search "Friends of Milford Upper Charles Trail."

GPS Coordinates: 42°09'22.28"N 71°31'12.66"W (Louisa Lake) 42°11'19.79"N 71°30'19.24"W (near Hopkinton line)

MILFORD

42°08'37.63"N 71°30'47.24"W (Fino Field) 42°08'55.15N 71°30'00.26"W (Friendly's)

Directions: Several trailheads:

Fino Field in downtown Milford off Rt. 16 (across the street from Sacred Heart of Jesus Catholic Church and Beach St.).

Louisa Lake on Dilla St. From Rt. 495 to exit 20, Rt. 85, travel south on Rt. 85 toward Milford, first right is Dilla St., with a Wendy's restaurant at the corner. Follow Dilla St. about 1 mile, and look for bike crossing signs.

Milford/Hopkinton Town Line Rt. 495, exit 20, travel north on Rt. 85 for 1.5 miles toward Hopkinton, parking is on right.

Friendly's Restaurant 495 to exit 19 Rt. 109, follow Rt. 109 toward Milford Center, to Friendly's Restaurant on left, or continue to Hannaford's Supermarket, also on left, (just before intersection with Rt. 16) trail is at back of parking area.

Cost: None.

Bathrooms: None, but there are many nearby downtown area businesses that may have available facilities.

Best Time to Visit: Year-round, but not plowed in winter.

Trail Conditions: Wide, paved rail-trail, mostly flat, with pedestrian-marked road crossings.

Distance: About 10 miles, from parking at the Hopkinton town line on Rt. 85 through downtown Milford, then up to Holliston

MILFORD

Center. Distance includes a section of the Upper Charles Trail-Holliston (details for Holliston section of this trail in *More Easy Walks in Massachusetts*).

Parking: Large paved parking on Rt. 85 at the Milford-Hopkinton town line for 20+ cars; at Louisa Lake on Dilla St. for 25+ cars; at Fino Field on Rt. 16, behind Hannaford supermarket on Rt. 109 and 16; and at Friendly's Rt. 109.

The Upper Charles Trail originates in downtown Milford. One branch travels northwest to Hopkinton's town line, while another branch travels northeast toward Holliston's town center. Close to 10 miles long (including the stonedust portion of Holliston's Upper Charles Trail), the paved Milford section of trail is part of a planned non-motor system that will eventually stretch from Milford to Framingham. The rail-trail crosses several streets, including the Rt. 85 exit at Rt. 495. Great care should be exercised when crossing at intersections, as these are busy roads.

Multiple water views of the Upper Charles River watershed are visible along the way. From Louisa Lake toward Rt. 495, keep an eye out for large boulders and remnants of granite quarrying operations. Look for portions of the Upper Charles, which feeds into Louisa Lake, just downstream from the headwaters of the Charles. The river originates at Echo Lake in Hopkinton, MA, quite near parking off Rt. 85 near the Hopkinton town line.

MILFORD

Near the downtown area the landscape is marshy, which attracts waterfowl. Signs warn about waterfowl hunting, so use caution during late fall months, and wear blaze orange!

From Fino Field, cross Rt. 16 at the light by the Sacred Heart of Jesus Catholic Church, go down Beach Street one block to Mt. Pleasant Street to pick up the Phase 3 portion of the Upper Charles Trail. This 1-mile section parallels Rt. 16 as it travels toward Hannaford supermarket parking and Friendly's restaurant.

Follow signs that will bring you around to Friendly's where the trail continues on the large sidewalk, up to where a crosswalk light is posted to aid walkers and bikers in crossing Rt. 109. Once across Rt. 109, head northeast toward the Holliston section of the Upper Charles Trail. At the Holliston line the surface becomes packed stonedust, not pavement. While some portions of the Holliston trail have a finished surface, additional portions are still under development.

Because this is such a popular trail, walkers as well as bikers must take care. If biking, give people verbal or bike-bell warnings when approaching. If walking, observe signs that indicate which side of the trail to stay on. Take care to keep children to one side.

"QR" codes are posted at the kiosks at trail entrances, accessed with smart phones. These codes provide trail maps, accessed through the Friends of Milford Upper Charles Trail Facebook page, which provides the most up-to-date trail information.

Millis

MILLIS

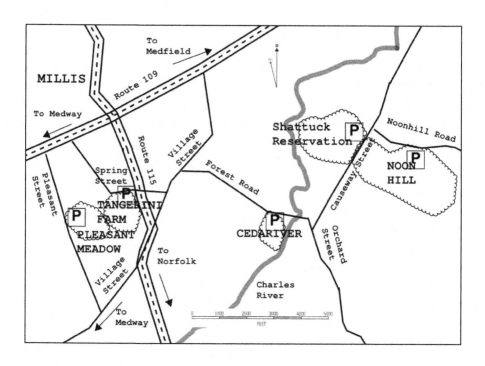

MILLIS

Cedariver

Features: Loop trail to the banks of the Upper Charles River.

Trail Map: Search "Cedariver Trustees of Reservation."

GPS Coordinates: 42°09'29.58"N 71°20'10.09"W

Directions: 161 Forest Road. From Millis Center, at the intersection of Rts. 115 and 109, head east 0.75 mile on Rt. 109 to a right onto Village St. Travel south on Village St. about 0.75 mile to a left at Forest Rd. Continue on Forest Rd 0.5 mile, look for the Cedariver sign on the right.

Cost: None.

Bathrooms: None.

Best Time to Visit: Year-round. Wear blaze orange in fall during hunting season, and mosquito repellant in warm months.

Trail Conditions: Unimproved, broad dirt track, trails well marked. Some inclines along trails.

Distance: About a 1-mile loop trail down to the banks of the Upper Charles River, and then back.

Parking: Small parking area at trail kiosk.

Cedariver offers great views of the Charles River, a canoe put-in to allow for travel on the river, along with a pleasant easy walk through open fields and woodland. We spotted numerous tree stumps chewed by beavers on our walk along the banks of the Charles. (A shy beaver cruised along the shoreline during our visit to this quiet spot.)

The open areas of fields are next to the river. This spot is a great place to search for birds. Staying out in the open is a good strategy for avoiding mosquitoes too!

Cedariver is quite near several additional properties owned by the Trustees of Reservations: Noon Hill and the Shattuck Reservation, Medfield; and Rocky Narrows, Sherborn.

MILLIS

While many Trustees of Reservations properties charge an entry fee, Cedariver is free to all. Dogs are welcome, but are limited to two dogs per person.

MILLIS

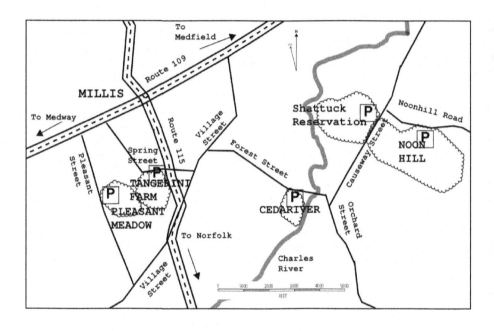

Tangerini Farm/Pleasant Meadow

Features: Farm is open May 1-Oct. 31, hiking trail through farm fields to adjacent open space at Pleasant Meadow.

Trail Map: Not presently available.

MILLIS

GPS Coordinates: 42°09'45.97"N 71°21'25.82"W (Tangerini Farm) 42°09'24.52"N 71°21'49.09"W (Pleasant Meadow).

Directions: **To farm**: From Millis Center, intersection of Rts. 115 and 109, head south on Rt. 115 for 0.5 mile toward Norfolk, turn right onto Spring St., and farm entrance is 0.1 mile on the left.

To Pleasant Meadow open space at 72 Pleasant St., Millis: From intersection of Rts. 115 and 109 in Millis center, head west on Rt. 109 toward Medway for 0.5 mile, turn left at light onto Pleasant St., 0.5 mile down look on left for small sign for the conservation property.

Cost: None. Ice cream, produce, and prepared foods are available for purchase seasonally at the farm stand.

Bathrooms: At Tangerini's Farm, available May 1-Oct. 31.

Best Time to Visit: Farm is open spring, summer and fall. The Pleasant Meadow access is not plowed in winter.

Trail Conditions: Farm trail is unmarked, wide, flat, open to the back of the farm toward woods where Pleasant Meadow adjoins property. Woodland trail is marked, mostly flat easy walking.

Distance: 1-1.5 miles hike depending on how much of the Pleasant Meadow trails are walked.

Parking: Gravel parking at Pleasant Meadow for 6-8 cars, gravel parking at Tangerini's Farm for 30+ cars.

MILLIS

Tangerini's Farm, accessed from Spring St. in Millis, offers CSA farm shares, pick-your-own fruits, vegetables, and flowers in season, as well as fresh produce, ice cream, and other foodstuffs at the farm stand. The public is welcome to walk at the farm. Its trails connect to the adjacent open space of Pleasant Meadow, which can also be accessed from Pleasant St.

Pleasant Meadow is a 37+-acre property, which provides a substantial corridor for wildlife combined with the farm next door. About 0.5 mile in length, the path at Pleasant Meadow offers several loops to follow that are all marked out with red, yellow or blue trail markers on trees, thanks to local Girl Scouts' efforts. This open space with its trails is open year-round, but the parking area may be blocked due to snow in winter.

When visiting Pleasant Meadow, enter through what appears to be a residential driveway to the graveled parking area. Once you're parked, look toward the wooded area for the "Trailhead" sign to begin your walk. A few trees have fallen across the paths, but nothing will be too difficult to step over. The open fields on either side of the wooded area are mowed by the Millis Conservation Commission to maintain habitat needed by bluebirds as well as other bird species. Dog walkers must clean up after their dogs.

MILLIS

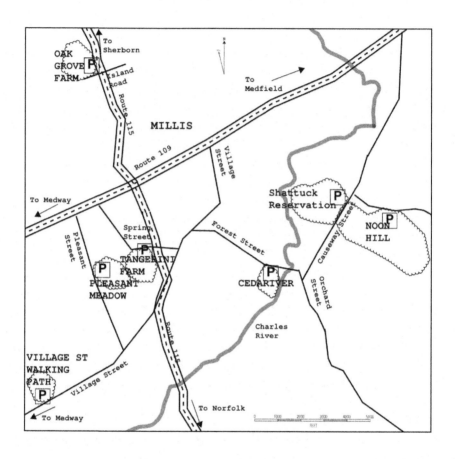

MILLIS

Village Street Walking Path

Features: Small wooded area with paths, adjacent open field.

Trail Map: None presently available.

GPS Coordinates: 42°08'30.30"N 71°22'21.48"W

Directions: From intersection of Rts. 109 and 115 in Millis, head west 0.5 mile on Rt. 109 to Pleasant St., then turn left at the light.

MILLIS

Travel south on Pleasant St. about 1 mile to a right onto Village St. Continue west on Village St. 0.8 mile, near 397 Village St., look for dirt parking on the right, small "Village Street Walking Path" sign set back at the edge of the parking area.

Cost: None.

Bathrooms: None.

Best Time to Visit: Year-round, though may be wet in spring.

Trail Conditions: Unimproved dirt path, boards through wet areas, fairly well marked, mostly quite level.

Distance: 0.75 loop trail.

Parking: Packed gravel parking area directly off Village St.

This small property provides a nice "edge community" that lends itself to bird watching. From Village St., walk across the open field to the woods. Within the wooded area a nice loop trail is laid out.

The property appears to get very wet in the spring. Several boardwalks in the woods are helpful for keeping feet dry over wet spots. The small open space sign on Village St. indicates rules and regulations. Horses are welcome except when fields are wet.

A raised railbed appears to provide an eastern border for this property and may provide additional areas for walking, but it has not been cleared or maintained. Thanks to Jennifer Powell, who pointed us to this sweet property.

MILLIS

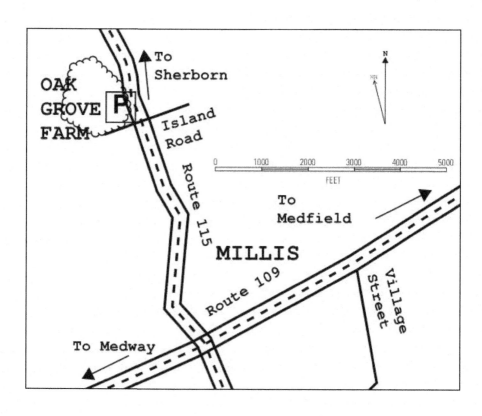

MILLIS

Oak Grove Farm

Features: Walking trails, community events.

Trail Map: Not presently available.

GPS Coordinates: 42°10'53.32"N 71°21'47.55"W

Directions: From Millis Center, at the intersection of Rts. 115 and 109, head north 1 mile on Rt. 115 toward Sherborn. Look for Oak Grove Farm on the left, just past Island Road.

MILLIS

Cost: None.

Bathrooms: Porta-potties in summer.

Best Time to Visit: Year-round.

Trail Conditions: Mowed paths in summer for walking through open farm fields.

Distance: 1-mile loop trail through farm field.

Parking: Gravel parking for 15 cars next to farmhouse.

Oak Grove Farm is a very popular spot for dog walkers as well as a great spot for community events in Millis. When we visited we found trails that had been mowed through the back field. The mowed paths made walking much easier, helping us avoid ticks that are a constant concern when walking in woodland as well as on grassy paths.

The farmhouse on the property dates back to the 17th century, and is now restored and managed by the Millis Historical Commission. The adjacent open fields are managed by the Oak Grove Farm Commission. Check local newspapers or town websites for upcoming events at this popular spot just outside Millis Center.

Millville

MILLVILLE

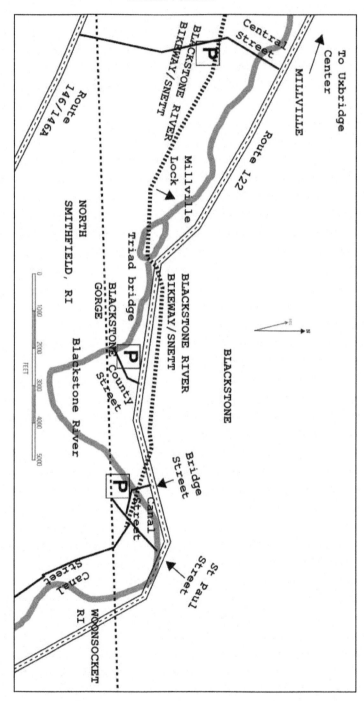

MILLVILLE

SNETT/Blackstone River Bikeway-Millville

Features: Paved rail-trail, Triad Bridge, and views of the Blackstone River, Millville Lock.

Trail Map: Search "DCR SNETT" then click on SNETT trail map.

GPS Coordinates: 42°01'26.41"N 71°34'57.48"W

Directions: From Rt. 16 in Uxbridge Center, drive south on Rt. 122 for 4.5 miles to Central St. in Millville, turn right, drive 0.25

MILLVILLE

mile on Central St., just past the stone church; parking is on the left.

Cost: None.

Bathrooms: None.

Best Time to Visit: Year-round.

Trail Conditions: Paved, wide (8-10 feet) rail-trail.

Distance: A 2-mile section in Millville is now paved. The Triad Bridge is still under construction as of press time, limiting travel onto the Blackstone section of the trail. Fall 2016, the Triad Bridge is scheduled for completion, which will allow for 4 total miles of travel on this paved rail-trail.

Parking: Paved parking lot adjacent to the trail on Central St. next to Stone Church, for 10-15 cars. There is an additional parking lot on 146A in Uxbridge, providing alternate access to this paved portion of the SNETT/Blackstone River Bikeway.

You'll find a whole lot to enjoy on this section of the SNETT, which travels concurrently with the Blackstone River Bikeway on this portion of the rail-trail. From Millville heading east toward Blackstone and the Triad Bridge, look on the left for the side trail that goes down to the river; take in the river views as well as the Millville Lock, the most intact remaining lock structure of the Blackstone Canal system.

MILLVILLE

Back on the trail, continue to the Triad Bridge, where three rail lines (two active, one proposed but never finished) crossed, stacked one on top of the other. Presently an active train line operates below the level of the rail-trail. The SNETT/Blackstone River Bikeway trail follows the path of the second train line. The bridge abutments to the south, on the Blackstone side of the bridge, are all that remains of the third planned rail line. Expect great views of the Blackstone River from the vantage point of this bridge, set upon a high spot above the Blackstone River.

This portion of the trail, heading both east and west from the parking on Central St. in Millville—as well as the bridge work over the river at the Triad Bridge—are all slated for completion in fall, 2016.

Northbridge

NORTHBRIDGE

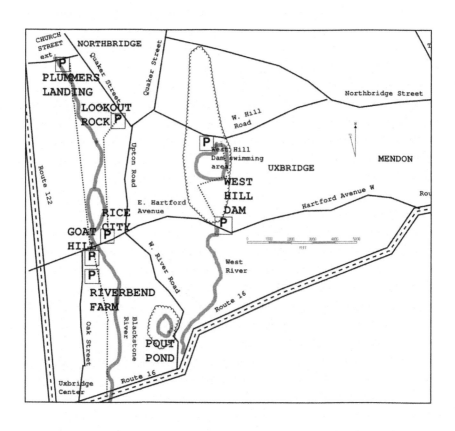

NORTHBRIDGE

Lookout Rock

Features: Views of Blackstone River Valley. Trailhead is east of the Blackstone River, and is an easy walk on unimproved trail to the views.

Trail Map: Search "DCR Riverbend Farm" click on downloadable map.

GPS Coordinates: 42°06'51.33"N 71°37'06.94"W

NORTHBRIDGE

<u>Directions:</u> From Mendon Center, intersection of Rt. 16 and North St., head west on Rt. 16; at 0.75 mile, turn right at Hartford Ave. (across from large auto dealerships in Mendon). Travel 2 miles to the West Hill Dam entrance in Uxbridge. Continue past West Hill Dam another 0.5 mile, turn right onto Upton Rd., travel 1 mile to the T at Quaker St. Turn left onto Quaker St., and look for the parking lot on the left, 0.1 mile.

<u>Cost:</u> None.

<u>Bathrooms:</u> None.

<u>Best Time to Visit:</u> Year-round, but note hunting is allowed in fall and early winter; wear blaze orange.

<u>Trail Conditions:</u> Unimproved dirt track, mostly level except for the scramble up onto Lookout Rock itself.

<u>Distance:</u> 0.2 mile from the parking to Lookout Rock.

<u>Parking:</u> Designated parking lot on Quaker Street for 4-6 cars.

Lookout Rock offers an unobstructed view of the Blackstone Valley, looking south and west from the vantage point of a prominent rock outcrop.

Plan on having a nice walk on easy paths to a broad view. You'll see a few signs of civilization when you get to the top of Lookout Rock. Ignore the intrusions and take in the view! From the parking area off Quaker St., look for a small sign "To Lookout Rock" on your right. The trails are pretty well marked, and only a

NORTHBRIDGE

little challenging in the fall when leaves cover the path. Upon arriving at the rock outcropping, use caution because of the substantial drop from the top of the rock to the ground below.

Refrain from tossing rocks from Lookout Rock, as there are numerous trails just below the lookout. Throwing rocks could cause serious injury to hikers who are walking below.

Trails below the rock lead back south along the east bank of the Blackstone River to Rice City Pond, Uxbridge. (See Uxbridge section, Rice City Pond in *Easy Walks*.)

NORTHBRIDGE

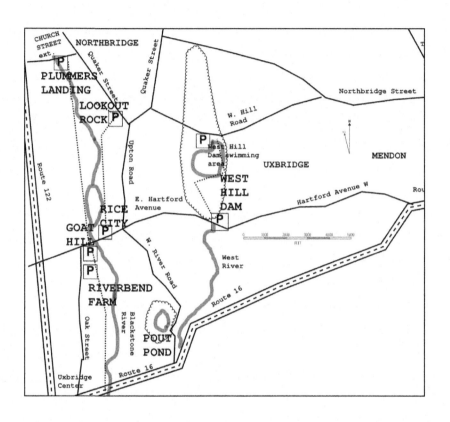

NORTHBRIDGE

Plummer's Landing

Features: Views of Blackstone River, unimproved dirt track alongside the Blackstone River Canal, and canoe put-in.

Trail Map: Search "DCR Riverbend Farm" click on downloadable map.

GPS Coordinates: 42°07'44.81"N 71°38'13.39"W

NORTHBRIDGE

Directions: At the intersection of Rt. 122 and Church St. Extension in Northbridge, turn right onto Church St. Extension, travel about 0.5 mile, and look for a parking area on the right; signs will indicate Plummer's Landing.

Cost: None.

Bathrooms: None.

Best Time to Visit: Year-round, and use insect repellant in spring and summer.

Trail Conditions: Rough, unimproved track. Trail may be quite overgrown in places, especially mid-way between Plummer's Landing and the Goat Hill trailhead.

Distance: About 2.25 miles from Plummer's Landing to the Goat Hill trailhead in Uxbridge.

Parking: Packed gravel designated parking.

While Plummer's Landing may have been a busy place at one time, it is now a rather quiet spot along the banks of the Blackstone River. The recreation area was named in memory of a store and inn owner who catered to the Blackstone Canal barge traffic that traveled through the area in the early 1800s.

Take a walk alongside the Blackstone Canal, which connects with the Goat Hill trail, accessed from Hartford Ave. in Uxbridge (See Uxbridge, Goat Hill section of *Easy Walks*).

NORTHBRIDGE

Expect to find some nice water views as you walk along the west bank of the Blackstone River and canal. A popular spot for dog walkers, it is also an area open for hunting. People and dogs must wear blaze orange during hunting season.

Upton

UPTON

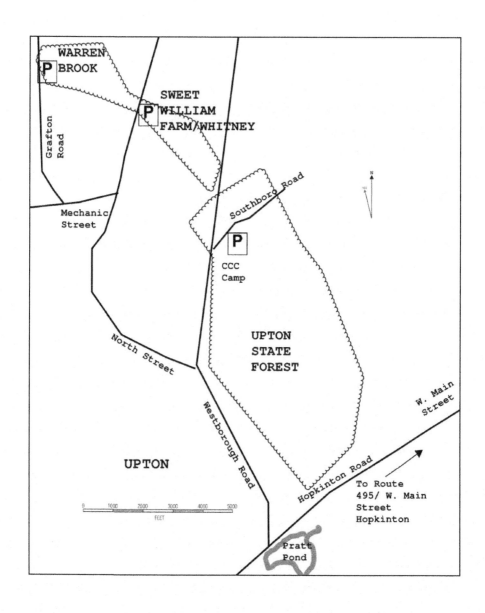

UPTON

CCC Camp Upton State Forest

Features: Water views, some flat, open fire roads, popular with horseback riders. Civilian Conservation Corps (CCC) Headquarters building. No metal detectors are permitted on state property.

Trail Map: At kiosk at trailhead, or search "DCR Upton State Forest."

GPS Coordinates: 42°12'33.75"N 71°36'32.27"W

UPTON

Directions: 205 Westborough Rd. From Rt. 495 to W. Main St., at Hopkinton/Upton exit 21, travel west 3.5 miles toward Upton. Turn right onto Westborough Rd., travel 1.5 miles to Southboro Rd., turn right, and parking is on the right.

Cost: None.

Bathrooms: Porta-potty at trailhead near CCC building, depending upon available funds.

Best Time to Visit: Year-round, though trail may be icy in winter.

Trail Conditions: Unimproved, wide, level dirt track, some rougher trails, some erosion, some trail markings.

Distance: Numerous loop trail options in this 2800-acre property (the approximate total acreage of the entire town-wide Upton State Forest holdings.)

Parking: Horse trailers can park in front of the CCC Building, and all visitors park in this area in the winter months. Otherwise, use packed gravel parking lot at the end of CCC Way, which is off of Southboro Rd.

The trails of the Upton State Forest, in the vicinity of the CCC Headquarters building, are a gift from the Great Depression. Out-of-work men were brought to the countryside for employment, building fire roads, bridges, and fire ponds. The headquarters building is the last remaining CCC headquarters building still standing in Massachusetts.

UPTON

This area is popular with horseback riders, skiers, hikers, and mountain bikers as well as those who simply want to spend some time outdoors. Impressive boulders are strewn throughout the woods; look for lady slippers blooming in season (June). Expect to find many other wildflowers and wildlife flourishing in this valuable open space. The State Forest offers challenging trails as well, but many sections feature flat, wide fire roads that are relatively level for easy walking with family and friends.

The Friends of the Upton State Forest are vigilant about land protection issues, working closely with other conservation organizations to assure that the State Forest will be there for future generations to enjoy. After ten years of effort by the Friends, the CCC Headquarters area, known as the "Upton State Forest Civilian Conservation Corps Resources Historic District" has been placed in the National Register of Historic Places.

Members of the Friends of the Upton State Forest were instrumental in helping gather the information for this edition of *Easy Walks*.

UPTON

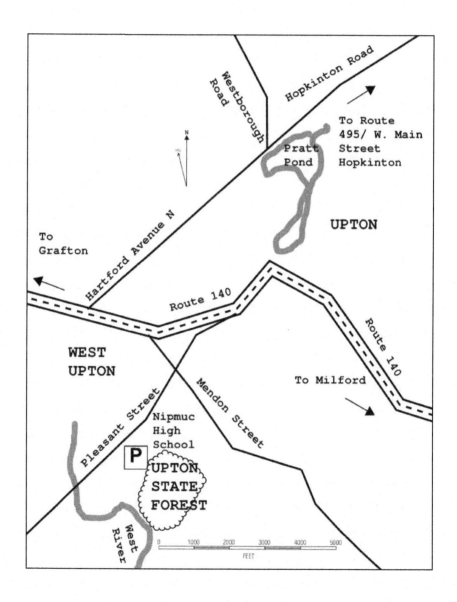

UPTON

Upton State Forest Pleasant St

Features: Wide, clear, unimproved dirt track, loop trail, unmarked. Water views of the West River. No metal detectors are permitted on state property.

Trail Map: None presently available.

GPS Coordinates: 42°09'29.22"N 71°37'01.13"W

UPTON

Directions: From Upton Center, Rt. 140, drive north toward West Upton 0.75 mile, to a left onto Pleasant St. Drive 1 mile on Pleasant St. to the back parking entrance of Nipmuc High School. Trailhead is at edge of the parking area.

Cost: None.

Bathrooms: None.

Best Time to Visit: After-school hours only during the school year. Trails are open to all when school is closed.

Trail Conditions: Unimproved, wide, level dirt track, no trail markings. A loop trail.

Distance: 1 mile loop trail to West River, then back to Nipmuc High school parking area.

Parking: Behind Nipmuc High School in the school parking lot after school hours only, and when school is closed.

Many state forests in Massachusetts towns consist of contiguous parcels, but Upton has a number of separate parcels of state forest land that comprise the Upton State Forest. This section of State Forest is accessed best directly behind Nipmuc High School off Pleasant St. in Upton. Thus, access is restricted when school is in session. Despite this restriction, it's a nice property to visit, and provides easy walking throughout the loop trail that takes you along the banks of the West River.

UPTON

We found signs of beaver activity along the edge of the river. Large red pine plantings are evident, remnants of efforts in the 1930s to make the forest a commercially viable enterprise. A clear track, the path is relatively easy to follow, with only a few side trails that lead into close-by neighborhoods, which may present some temporary confusion for hikers.

UPTON

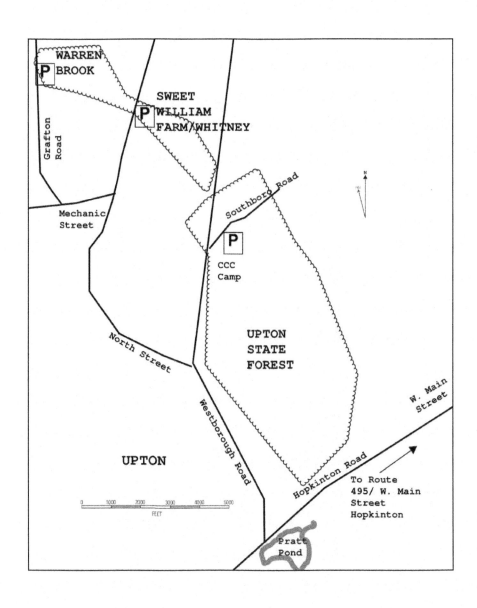

UPTON

Whitney Conservation Area

Features: Unimproved marked trails, meadow views, stone walls, farm views.

Trail Map: Search "Upton MA Conservation land," click on Whitney Conservation area map.

GPS Coordinates: 42°12'56.21"N 71°37'15.64"W

UPTON

Directions: 147 North St., Upton. From Rt. 495 to W. Main St., Hopkinton/Upton exit 21, travel west 3.5 miles on W. Main St. (becomes Hopkinton Rd. in Upton) toward Upton. Turn right onto Westborough Rd., travel 2.25 miles to a left onto North St. Travel on North St. 1.2 miles to 147 North St. where parking is on the right.

Cost: None

Bathrooms: None available.

Best time to visit: Year-round.

Trail conditions: Cart paths, a few wet spots. Can be very wet in the spring.

Distance: 1-mile loop, numerous additional options connecting with Upton State Forest, Warren Brook conservation area.

Parking: Packed gravel marked parking area at 147 North St.

Sweet William Farm/Whitney Conservation Area has a lovely view of an open meadow directly across the street from the parking area on North St. Choose from a couple of hiking options at this spot: head away from the street upland, following the double stone wall that marks the edge of the parking area, or cross the street to head downhill on the Whitney property toward Warren Brook.

A short, 1-mile loop trail is available upland, following the stone wall past the farm fields. Beware of the electric fencing next

UPTON

to the trail, placed to prevent deer depredations on the crops. The fence may be live, with potential for injury.

Several spurs branch off the main trail. One heads off to the right back toward an access trail south of the parking area, which comes out in a nearby neighborhood. Other options include continuing on to the Upton State Forest lands, which are adjacent to this conservation area. Or you can follow the signs (or the map) to circle back for a simple 1-mile loop excursion.

Heading downhill toward Warren Brook, look for stone walls, piney woods, and some fairly steep trails that eventually connect to the Warren Brook property. No loop trail is available presently, but there are plans to create a small loop trail for those looking for an easier walk.

UPTON

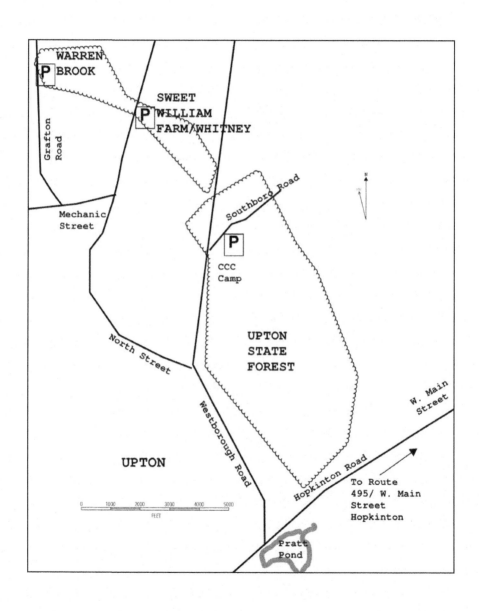

UPTON

Warren Brook

Features: Woodland walk on unimproved dirt track, loop trail available, longer treks possible with connections to Whitney Conservation Area.

Trail Map: Search "Upton Conservation Land," click on Warren Brook Conservation map.

GPS Coordinates: 42°12'04.06"N 71°38'25.40"W

UPTON

Directions: From Rt. 495 to W. Main St. at Hopkinton/Upton exit 21, travel west 3.5 miles on W. Main St. (becomes Hopkinton Rd. in Upton) toward Upton. Turn right onto Westborough Rd., and travel 2.25 miles to the left onto North St. Travel 0.75 mile on North St. to a left onto Mechanic St. Drive 0.1 mile on Mechanic St. to a right onto Grafton Rd. Travel 0.8 mile on Grafton Rd. to the trailhead.

Cost: None.

Bathrooms: None.

Best Time to Visit: Year-round, and use insect repellant in spring and summer.

Trail Conditions: Rough, unimproved dirt track.

Distance: Multiple trails, from the 1-mile loop to much longer distances, including connecting trails in the Whitney Conservation Area, Howarth Glen, and Upton State Forest property.

Parking: Packed gravel designated parking for 3-4 cars is directly off Grafton Rd.; a large sign is posted at the parking area.

Warren Brook offers some wide, open paths for easy walks through woodland. Some rock outcrops add interest to the walk. There are many stone walls, with lots of quiet in this conservation area.

A nice loop trail is laid out through the woodland. One small bridge makes hiking easier in the spring, when the property tends

UPTON

to be wet. For those looking for more ambitious walks, this property connects with the Whitney Conservation Area, but please be aware that the connecting trails are rather rough and challenging—not an easy walk!

UPTON

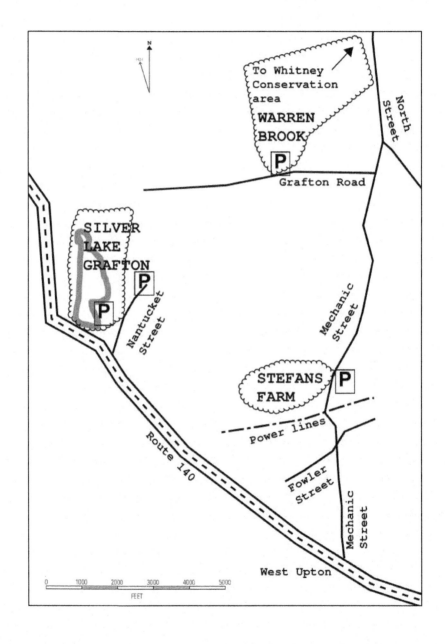

UPTON

Stefans Farm

Features: Wide unimproved dirt track, views from the top of the farm field.

Trail Map: Search "Upton Conservation Land," then Stefans Farm.

GPS Coordinates: 42°11'15.53"N 71°37'43.97"W

UPTON

Directions: From Upton Center, travel north on Rt. 140 to West Upton 1 mile to Hartford Ave. Continue north (toward Grafton) another 0.5 mile to Mechanic St. on the right. Travel on Mechanic St. 1 mile to parking on the right for Stephans Farm, just past power lines. Trailhead is directly across the street from parking and the Upton Community Garden area.

Cost: None.

Bathrooms: None.

Best Time to Visit: Year-round. Use insect repellant in spring and summer.

Trail Conditions: Rough, unimproved track.

Distance: A 1-mile loop trail, with many additional trails on the property.

Parking: Large, gravel parking area on Mechanic St., directly across the street from the marked trailhead.

Stefan's Farm has an initial steep climb but it's only for a few yards, before the path eases out into an easy walk through large, former farm fields. Stop to look back behind you to take in some great views of Upton as you climb higher through the farm fields.

This property has loop trails available, but the loop along the stone walls to the left of the farm field is rougher than recommended for an easy walk. For more comfortable walking, stay to the right in the main farm track. The track eventually bears to the left, but making a loop requires travel over some very rough paths.

If you find yourself at the power lines, you've gotten off the property—be advised to turn back! Do not attempt to find your way down along the power lines; the track is very rough, and will be blocked by fencing and other obstacles.

Additional trails on the same side of the street as the parking area lead past the community gardens area. Look for woodcocks courting in this area in the spring.

Uxbridge

UXBRIDGE

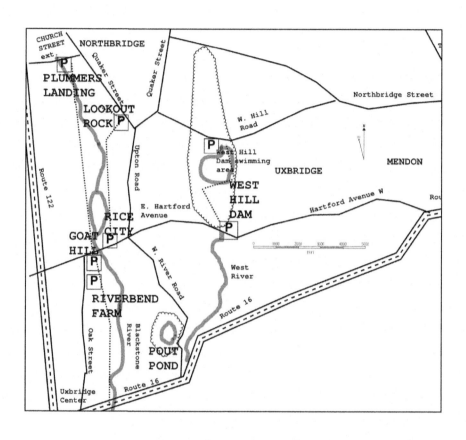

UXBRIDGE

River Bend Farm

Features: Hard-packed gravel path, the original towpath for the historic Blackstone River Canal; stone arched bridges at Hartford Ave.; remnants of locks along the canal route. The trailhead is west of the Blackstone River. Handicapped-accessible visitor's center, and the trail is handicapped friendly.

Trail Map: Search "DCR Riverbend Farm"

UXBRIDGE

GPS Coordinates: 42°05'38.82"N 71°37'25.46"W

Directions: Address: 287 Oak St., Uxbridge. From Mendon Center, intersection of Rt. 16, North and Main Sts., head west on Rt. 16. At 0.75 mile, turn right at Hartford Ave. (across from large auto dealerships in Mendon), then travel 2 miles to West Hill Dam entrance in Uxbridge. Pass West Hill Dam, another 0.5 mile, pass signs for Rice City Pond parking, and cross narrow bridge. Oak St. is almost immediately past the bridge. Turn left onto Oak St., travel 0.1 mile, and look for the visitor's center, a large red barn on the left.

Cost: None.

Bathrooms: Handicapped-accessible bathrooms at visitor's center, open 365 days a year.

Best Time to Visit: Year-round.

Trail Conditions: Unimproved flat towpath. Additional trails are unimproved dirt tracks.

Distance: Canal towpath next to farm, from Hartford Ave. to Rt. 16 Stanley Woolen Mill, 1 mile. Additional trails are north of Hartford Ave., along both the east and west banks of the Blackstone River.

Parking: Paved parking for 15 cars next to the visitor's center, with additional parking on the adjacent lawn for special events; additional parking at the back of Tri-River Medical Center on Hartford Ave.

UXBRIDGE

River Bend Farm is one of the designated visitor's centers for the Blackstone River Valley National Historical Park. The towpath adjacent to Riverbend Farm provides easy walking. No fences or railings stand between the path and canal, which in places has a steep embankment.

The canal beside the visitor's center offers canoe and kayak access. Additional, less-traveled paths follow the banks of the Blackstone River itself. From the Visitor's Center, cross the bridge to the towpath, turn either left or right to walk the towpath itself, or go almost straight across the towpath bridge onto trails along the edge of a large field opposite the Visitor's Center. Then head toward the river, on your left as you face the field.

Two arched stone bridges at the north end of the towpath at Hartford Ave., under which the Blackstone River flows, offer a perfect spot for group photos. The Blackstone River tends to run quite high in the spring, but generally is much quieter during the rest of the year. Benches along the towpath offer resting spots for weary walkers. Several remnants of locks remain along this towpath.

Rice City Pond, Goat Hill on the west banks of the Blackstone, Plummer's Landing (west bank of the Blackstone), and Lookout Rock (Northbridge) all link to each other, accessible on foot from any single parking location for the more enterprising walker.

UXBRIDGE

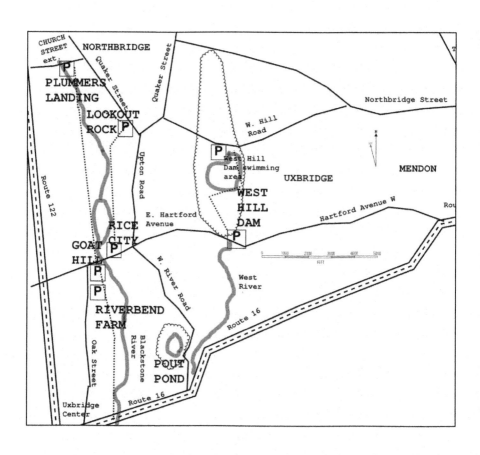

UXBRIDGE

Goat Hill

Features: Packed dirt unimproved track, Blackstone River canal lock remnants, some large boulders along the trail. Additional, more challenging trails up Goat Hill. Trail is west of the Blackstone River, and connects with Plummer's Landing (Northbridge) by traveling north along banks of the Blackstone.

UXBRIDGE

Trail Map: Search "DCR Riverbend Farm, then click on downloadable map.

GPS Coordinates: 42°05'53.74"N 71°37'27.64"W

Directions: From Mendon Center, intersection of Rt. 16, North and Main Sts., head west on Rt. 16. At 0.75 mile, turn right at Hartford Ave. (across from large auto dealerships in Mendon) then travel 2 miles to West Hill Dam entrance in Uxbridge. Pass West Hill Dam, another 0.5 mile, pass signs for Rice City Pond parking, and cross the narrow bridge. Just past the bridge, look on the right for the trailhead.

Cost: None.

Bathrooms: At River Bend Farm year-round.

Best Time to Visit: Year-round.

Trail Conditions: Unimproved dirt track, mostly level.

Distance: 0.3 mile to canal lock, 2+ miles to reach Plummer's Landing in Northbridge.

Parking: Park at River Bend Farm or at Tri-River Medical Center 280 Hartford Ave., then cross Hartford Ave. Do not park directly on the road in front of the trail kiosk; a private driveway is right next to the property.

It is possible to track remnants of the Blackstone Canal towpath as you walk this trail, but on this section of trail the towpath itself is

UXBRIDGE

overgrown. Abandoned nearly 150 years ago, much of the canal and towpath have washed away, leaving only a few places where the towpath can still be seen. Look for the curious, straight, long spit of land a few feet off shore on your right as you travel north.

Access is available to a rare view of a canal lock, which was used to raise or lower water levels along the canal when it was in operation from the 1820s to the 1840s. Cargo was transported from Worcester to Pawtucket through the Blackstone Canal. About 0.3 mile from Hartford Ave. along the path, look for signs on the right that point to the lock. It's a steep scramble down off the main path, but worth the effort. A wooden bridge leads to the towpath and lock. After crossing the bridge, examine each end of the lock carefully. Granite blocks still frame the channel the boats traversed, and wooden sluice gates were raised or lowered to alter the water level so boats could safely travel up or down the river despite changes in elevation.

Named for the hill that rises steeply from the banks of Rice City Pond, Goat Hill trail offers additional trails that circle Goat Hill itself. This is a popular area, so trails tend to be icy in the winter because of heavy foot traffic. Along the river the path is open for quite some distance, but eventually becomes more difficult to travel as it heads toward Plummer's Landing, Northbridge. Trees prevent a clear view of the water. For better views, Lookout Rock (See Northbridge-Lookout Rock section in *Easy Walks*) can be reached from the east side of the river.

UXBRIDGE

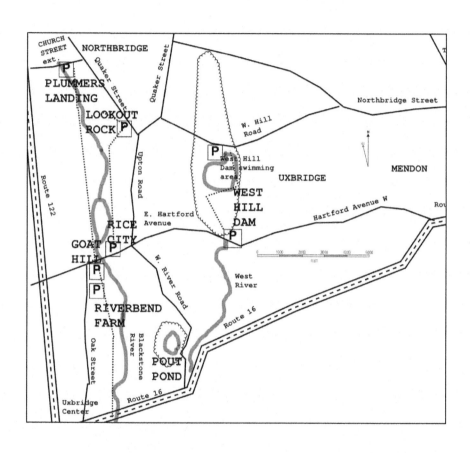

UXBRIDGE

Rice City Pond

Features: Narrow, unimproved dirt track with views along east side of the Blackstone River; and wildlife. The trailhead is on the east bank of Blackstone River, and leads to base of Lookout Rock (see Northbridge section of *Easy Walks*).

Trail Map: Search "DCR Riverbend Farm," downloadable map.

GPS Coordinates: 42°05'58.60"N 71°37'09.59"W

UXBRIDGE

Directions: From Mendon Center, intersection of Rt. 16 and North St., head west on Rt. 16. At 0.75 mile turn right at Hartford Ave. (across from large auto dealerships in Mendon), travel 2 miles to the West Hill Dam entrance in Uxbridge. Pass West Hill Dam, and go another 0.5 mile. Just before the Blackstone River, look on the right for signs for Rice City Pond parking.

Cost: None.

Bathrooms: None.

Best Time to Visit: Year-round. Parking may not be plowed in winter.

Trail Conditions: Unimproved dirt track, mostly level, narrow in places along river. Becomes quite steep in the approach to Lookout Rock

Distance: 1 mile from parking at Hartford Ave. to Lookout Rock, just off Quaker St., Northbridge.

Parking: A packed-gravel designated parking area is directly off Hartford Avenue.

The east side of the Blackstone River at this area offers picnic tables, canoe access to the river, and a trail that travels north alongside the east bank of the Blackstone. The foot trail from Rice City Pond eventually leads all the way to Lookout Rock if you continue to follow the riverbank for about 1 mile; the path is somewhat narrow and sloped in places. While walking, you may

UXBRIDGE

see turtles sunning themselves in shallow water, or resting on fallen logs in the (usually) slow-flowing river. Look for signs of muskrats.

A stone bridge crosses the Blackstone River just past the parking area, with additional trails on the west side of the river both to the north and the south of Hartford Ave. (River Bend Farm and Goat Hill). The approach to Lookout Rock from this trail is quite steep. Take care, as the eroded trails can be very slippery.

UXBRIDGE

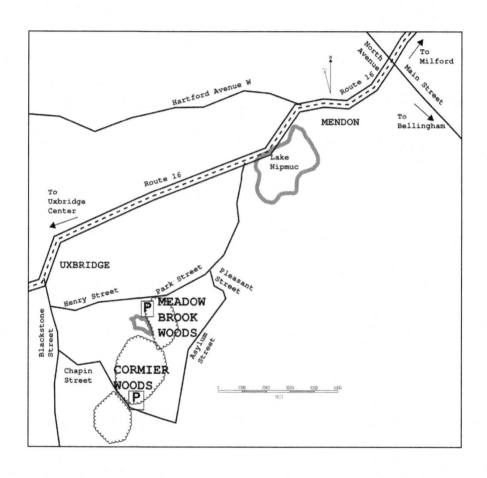

UXBRIDGE

Cormier Woods

Features: Trustees of Reservations property, marked, unimproved dirt trails, variable elevations, restored historical barn, old stone foundations, and stone walls. A Trustees of Reservations property, so hunting is permitted.

Trail Map: At trailhead kiosk or search "Trustees of Reservations Cormier Woods."

UXBRIDGE

GPS Coordinates: 42°04'09.96"N 71°35'40.94"W

Directions: From Mendon Center, travel west on Rt. 16 for 3.2 miles to Blackstone St. (Welcome to Uxbridge sign in triangle on the left). Turn left onto Blackstone St., travel 0.5 mile to a left onto Chapin St. Cormier Woods parking is on the left, 0.75 mile down on Chapin St.

Cost: Free for Trustees of Reservations members; $4 donation requested from visitors.

Bathrooms: None.

Best Time to Visit: Year-round. The Trustees permits hunting, so be sure to wear blaze orange during hunting season.

Trail Conditions: Rough, narrow, dirt track, but mostly clear trail markings. On the opposite side of Chapin St. from parking area, additional trails lead through the woods; the topography is rather steep in places. Use caution when walking these trails.

Distance: Multiple loop trails available, with most under 2 miles.

Parking: Parking for 6-8 cars in packed-gravel designated lot.

Trails at Cormier Woods (along with Meadow Brook Woods in Mendon) are still being developed. Cormier Woods has connecting trails to Meadow Brook Woods (See Mendon—Meadow Brook Woods in *Easy Walks*) which is another property overseen by The Trustees of Reservations, adjacent to Cormier Woods. These connecting trails provide the more ambitious hiker with substantial

UXBRIDGE

additional areas to explore, including links to the Mendon Town Forest (very poorly marked).

Stone walls, abandoned house foundations, and old barn foundations all indicate that this property was a working farm in the 1800s. Stone foundations offer intriguing clues to past land use at Cormier Woods. Trails lead into woods on either side of Chapin St., which bisects this property.

UXBRIDGE

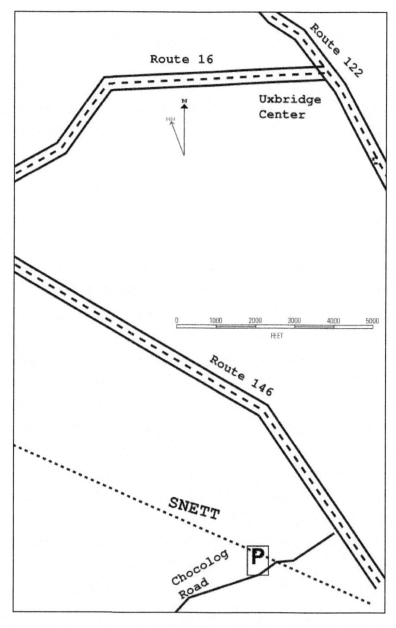

UXBRIDGE

SNETT Uxbridge

Features: Rock cuts, pond, very walkable, undeveloped rail-trail that continues to Douglas State Forest.

Trail Map: Search "DCR SNETT Uxbridge" then click on SNETT map.

UXBRIDGE

GPS Coordinates: 42°02'34.53"N 71°38'7.87"W

Directions: From Uxbridge Center take Rt. 16 west 2 miles to Rt. 146 south; travel 2 miles south to the Chocolog Rd. exit, turn right onto Chocolog Rd.; at the fork at 0.25 mile, bear left to stay on Chocolog another 0.1 mile. Look for SNETT road signs, and crossing gates for SNETT. Parking is along the road. SNETT is on both sides of Chocolog Rd.

Cost: None.

Bathrooms: None.

Best Time to Visit: Year-round.

Trail Conditions: Unimproved, wide, graded dirt track railbed; open, relatively flat, some sandy spots.

Distance: 3 miles west to Douglas State Forest, 1.5 miles east, blocked by Rt. 146. There is presently no access east to other sections of the SNETT across the highway.

Parking: Very limited pull-off areas are next to the road at the trailhead. Do not block the gate.

The proposed SNETT originates in Franklin, MA, and travels to Douglas, passing through Bellingham, Blackstone, Millville, and Uxbridge before its terminus in Douglas State Park. This section of the SNETT has very few grade crossings and limited parking access, but allows for an pleasant ride when traveling by bike or horseback. It is also popular with local dog walkers.

UXBRIDGE

The path is broad and level, with some examples of interesting stonework in the retaining walls, which were constructed when the railroad was built. Look for a pond on the north side of the trail. You'll find interesting stonework in the culvert that runs underneath the railbed.

For better access with more generous parking, venture farther west into Douglas to the parking areas indicated on the map in the Douglas portion of this book.

UXBRIDGE

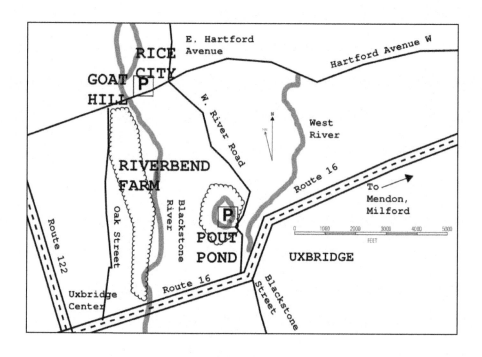

UXBRIDGE

Pout Pond

Features: Seasonal swimming area, no lifeguards, trails in woodland area.

Trail Map: None available.

GPS Coordinates: 42°05'11.08"N 71°36'29.99"W

UXBRIDGE

Directions: Travel west on Rt. 16 from Mendon Center for 3.5 miles to West River Rd. in Uxbridge. Turn right onto West River Rd. and continue about 0.5 mile, then look for an athletic field and the Pout Pond entrance, both on the left.

Cost: Daily fee charged, May-August.

Bathrooms: Available seasonally.

Best Time to Visit: Year-round.

Trail Conditions: Broad, clear, relatively level, unimproved track.

Distance: Not a loop trail around the pond, but a 1-mile series of trails near the pond.

Parking: Paved parking area, with the gate open year-round.

Trails adjacent to Pout Pond with several access points near the pond provide lots of options for easy walks. We found solid footing around the edge of the pond. Paths are comfortable, broad, relatively level, easy to follow, and offer nice views of the pond from different vantage points.

This town swimming area is for Uxbridge residents, with a nice sandy beach area next to the pond, but there are no lifeguards posted. Canoes and kayaks, as well as fishing, are permitted, but no motorized boats are permitted.

UXBRIDGE

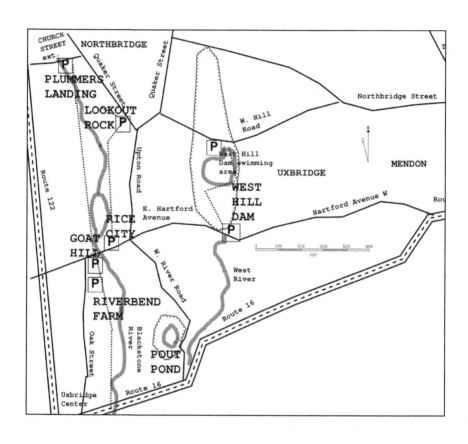

UXBRIDGE

West Hill Dam

Features: Easy, mostly level trails along unimproved dirt tracks, varied landscape, large dam, open, sunny fields, swimming area, and wildlife. Trailhead is east of the Blackstone River, with loop

UXBRIDGE

trails. Second entrance is open only in summer, to swimming area on West Hill Road, Northbridge.

Trail Map: At kiosk near swimming area, at headquarters building when open, near parking area next to dam, or search "Army Corps Engineers New England" then Recreation, West Hill Dam.

GPS Coordinates: 42°6'8.01"N 71°36'28.14"W (dam area) 42°6'45.95"N 71°36'15.66"W (swimming area).

Directions: Address: 518 East Hartford Ave. Uxbridge. From Mendon Center, the intersection of Rt. 16 and North St., head west on Rt. 16. At 0.75 mile, turn right onto E. Hartford Ave. (across from large auto dealerships in Mendon) then travel 2 miles to West Hill Dam entrance in Uxbridge on the right.

Cost: Free if you park at the dam. For the park, there is $1 fee per person over 13, with a maximum $4 charge per carload in summer

Bathrooms: At the ranger station. Also porta-potties are available near the dam area. Seasonally available at the swimming area.

Best Time to Visit: Dam area is open year-round; the parking lot is plowed in winter; and the swimming area is open in summer only.

Trail Conditions: Unimproved dirt track, roots, rocks on the trail between the dam and swimming area. Some open fields, packed gravel path along the top of the dam itself.

Distance: From dam to swimming area through the woods at end of dam is 0.5 mile. Path from mid dam though open fields to swimming are, 0.5 miles. Path west of dam through woods circles

UXBRIDGE

to swimming area. Loop trails of up to 2 miles available. Additional trails north of the swimming area are more challenging, recently cleared and marked. Download map for important trail information.

Parking: Paved parking for 25 cars next to the dam, and paved parking for 30 cars near swimming area.

After parking at the Hartford Ave. entrance, continue straight into the woods to follow the trail, or stop to investigate the dam itself. A small sluiceway is on the right. Porta-potties are near the sluiceway.

A walk along the top of the dam provides views of a wetlands area. At the end of the dam a trail leads into the woods, where you'll find seasonal streams as well as huge boulders. Keep an eye out for rocks and tree roots in the path.

The woods trail that begins below the dam brings you to the swimming area, loops around through woodland, on to open fields, and then back to the dam. No fee is charged if you enter the swimming area by this route in the summer, a half-mile walk.

At the entrance to the swimming area, accessed from West Hill Rd. in Uxbridge, a trail kiosk with maps indicates the location of additional trails. Trails are newly marked, so keep an eye out for trail markers and check out additional trails on the north side of the pond/swimming area.

Hunting season is from October 16 to April 1. Wear blaze orange, since the West Hill Dam area is open for hunting. No

UXBRIDGE

hunting is allowed in Massachusetts on Sundays. West Hill Dam in Uxbridge is maintained by the U.S. Army Corps of Engineers. The parking lot at E. Hartford Ave. is plowed in winter. Set aside for flood control, West Hill Dam has become a nature preserve filled with trails.

At the West Hill Park swimming area, children under 10 *must* be accompanied by parents, guardians, or other adults. No lifeguards are ever posted. The park season begins the third Saturday of May, and closes the second Sunday of September. No dogs are allowed at the swimming area, per the Board of Health.

Call the ranger's office at 508-278-2511 for more information. West Hill Dam offers family-oriented nature programs throughout the year.

Wrentham

WRENTHAM

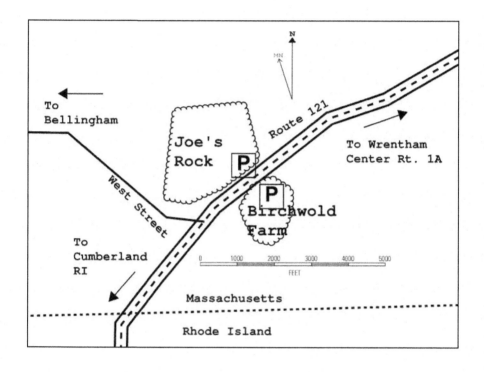

WRENTHAM

Joe's Rock

Features: Rough, unimproved track with washed out waterbar steps to top of Joe's Rock, views of the surrounding countryside from the top of Joe's Rock. Migrating waterfowl in the pond below Joe's Rock in spring and fall. Additional trails below the rock and alongside the pond.

WRENTHAM

Trail Map: Search "Wrentham Conservation land," download the pdf that includes a map of Joe's Rock and other conservation properties.

GPS Coordinates: 42°01'45.02"N 71°24'24.95"W

Directions: **From Wrentham Center**: from Wrentham Town Common Rt. 140, take 1A south 1.5 miles to the intersection with Rt. 121. Take the right fork to follow Rt. 121 into the Sheldonville area of Wrentham for 3.5 miles, and look for a large sign on the right for Joe's Rock.

From Bellingham direction: from Rt. 126 Crooks Corner, (corner of Rt. 126 and Pulaski Blvd.) take Paine St. for 0.1 mile, fork left onto Wrentham Rd. (which becomes West St. in Wrentham), travel 4.5 miles to a T with Rt. 121, and turn left onto Rt. 121. Birchwold Farm is on the right about 100 yards, with Joe's Rock on the left.

Cost: None.

Bathrooms: None.

Best Time to Visit: Year-round, but icy in winter climbing to top of Joe's Rock.

Trail Conditions: Unimproved dirt track. The trail alongside the pond at Joe's Rock has many roots—tripping hazards! The trail up to Joe's Rock is steep in places, with waterbar steps washed out to a large extent. A challenging climb.

WRENTHAM

Distance: To the top of Joe's Rock, 0.5 mile; along the edge of the pond, 0.5 mile; below Joe's Rock, 0.5 mile.

Parking: Paved parking area for 5-6 cars at Joe's Rock.

At 490 feet elevation, Joe's Rock provides a view northeast toward Boston, and southwest over the Rhode Island countryside. Next to the parking area, the path crosses a small stream that must be traversed by walking along a foot-wide board. Then immediately fork right or left. The right fork heads to the top of Joe's Rock, the left, or southern, fork meanders along the shore of the pond. Additional trails travel below Joe's Rock on the north side of the pond.

Numerous tree roots offer tripping hazards, while the steep, somewhat washed-out waterbars offer some challenging footing en route to the top of Joe's Rock. (Interest in Joe's Rock is what originally prompted me to create this travel guide.) Here's hoping you have a great trek!

WRENTHAM

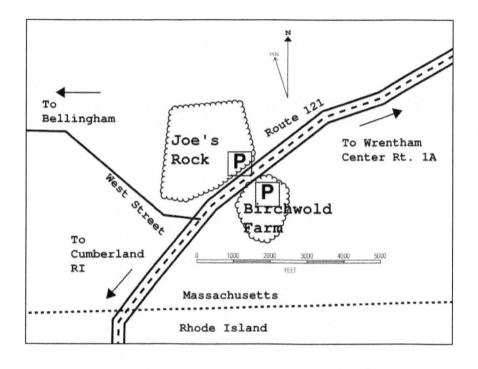

Birchwold Farm

Features: Clear, unimproved dirt tracks, with some trail markings, broad open fields at Birchwold Farm, and woodcock courtship flights in spring.

Trail Map: Search "Wrentham Conservation land," download the pdf that includes map of Joe's Rock and other conservation properties.

GPS Coordinates: 42°01'45.02"N 71°24'24.95"W

WRENTHAM

Directions: **From Wrentham Center:** from Wrentham town common Rt. 140, take 1A south 1.5 miles to intersection with Rt. 121. Take the right fork to follow Rt. 121 into the Sheldonville area of Wrentham for 3.5 miles, and look for a large sign on the right for Joe's Rock.

From Bellingham direction: from Rt. 126 Crooks Corner, (corner of Rt. 126 and Pulaski Blvd.) take Paine St. for 0.1 mile, fork left onto Wrentham Rd. (which becomes West St. in Wrentham) travel 4.5 miles to a T with Rt. 121, turn left onto Rt. 121. Birchwold Farm is on right about 100 yards, with Joe's Rock on the left.

Cost: None.

Bathrooms: None.

Best Time to Visit: Year-round.

Trail Conditions: Unimproved dirt track.

Distance: You can either walk the edge of the farm field, or take the woods trails out to power lines, and then back in a loop, about 1.5 miles.

Parking: Packed gravel, lots of potholes, very rough, for 10-15 cars.

Birchwold Farm offers a bright, sunny spot to walk out in the open year-round. The former dairy farm pasture had gotten somewhat overgrown the past few years, but was recently cut back. Visitors

WRENTHAM

now get a wide-open vista along well-worn paths, on the edge of and crisscrossing the open field.

Additional trails lead off from the open pasture into woods at several points along the way as you walk the circumference of the field. A bridge in the woods offers dry footing across a small stream that flows through the property.

Keep an eye out for rock outcroppings in the woods, as well as several trails that lead out to the power lines. Trails on the opposite side of the power lines loop back to a spot that once again crosses the stream through the woods. Crossing the water is possible by (carefully) using tree roots that grow over the stream.

Woodcocks are known to perform their courtship rituals on the edge of the open field at Birchwold Farm. For a chance to see this glorious courtship display, be sure to arrive at dusk on early spring evenings when you visit this 129-acre conservation property.

Trails are usable for horseback riding (or walking, of course!). Additional connected trails may traverse private property. Respect all notations of private property.

WRENTHAM

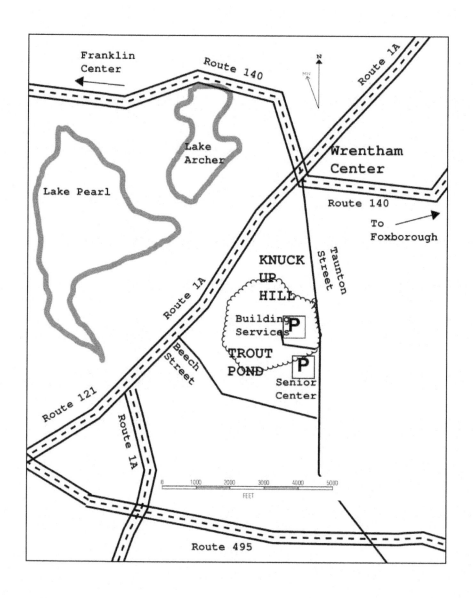

WRENTHAM

Knuckup Hill

Features: Wide, packed gravel fire road to the top of the hill, with views of the Boston skyline on clear days when leaves are down in the fall. A short, steep climb.

Trail Map: Search "Wrentham Conservation land," then download a pdf that contains maps of multiple conservation properties in Wrentham.

WRENTHAM

<u>GPS Coordinates:</u> 42°03'9.67"N 71°19'36.39"W

<u>Directions:</u> 400 Taunton St. Wrentham.

From Wrentham Center Rt. 140: traverse the town common to Taunton St. Travel south about 1 mile past the schools complex, and then look for Wrentham Senior Center on the right. Park at the senior center, or take fork to the right to the access road 0.2 miles to the Building Services Department, 350 Wrentham Road, past the senior center.

From Rt. 495: take Exit 15 (1A) north for 0.75 mile to the intersection with Rt. 121. Continue north on 1A for 0.3 mile, look for Beach St. on the right. Follow Beach St. 1 mile to the T with Taunton St., and turn left. Wrentham Senior Center is on the left about 0.3 mile farther on Taunton St. Park at the senior center, or continue past the senior center to the access road on the north side of the senior center, take the fork to the right toward the Building Services offices 0.2 mile, and park on the side of the road.

<u>Cost:</u> None.

<u>Bathrooms:</u> Available at the senior center when open.

<u>Best Time to Visit:</u> Year-round.

<u>Trail Conditions:</u> Unimproved packed gravel fire road, relatively wide. Additional woodland trails, unimproved dirt tracks.

<u>Distance:</u> 0.5 mile to the view.

<u>Parking:</u> Either at the senior center, or continue past the senior center on the Building Services Department access road and park

alongside the road, next to the Building Services offices, at the base of Knuckup Hill and within view of Trout Pond (also listed in *Easy Walks*).

On clear winter days (when the trees are bare) you can easily spot the office towers of downtown Boston by standing to the far left at the top of Knuckup Hill; look to the far right.

One trailhead begins on the right when you're facing the senior center, about 20 yards back from Taunton St. A "Warner Trail" sign indicates this is part of a larger trail system that travels from Canton into Connecticut. At this location, you can head into the woods on a path that is relatively flat until it joins what is clearly a gravel fire road. This fire road goes to the top of Knuckup Hill.

After reaching the fire road, head uphill, and continue till you're near the top of the hill. A smaller foot-trail branches off to the right, which quickly leads to a clearing. There, you'll see remnants of old ski lift equipment, and then the view!

Parking next to the Building Services Department and Trout Pond reduces your hike through woodland, offering a route straight up the fire road to the top of Knuckup Hill. Simply follow the fire road to the top of the hill, watch for the abandoned ski-lift mechanism, and then step off the fire road into the clearing to the right, where the view opens up. Beware of poison ivy throughout the area!

WRENTHAM

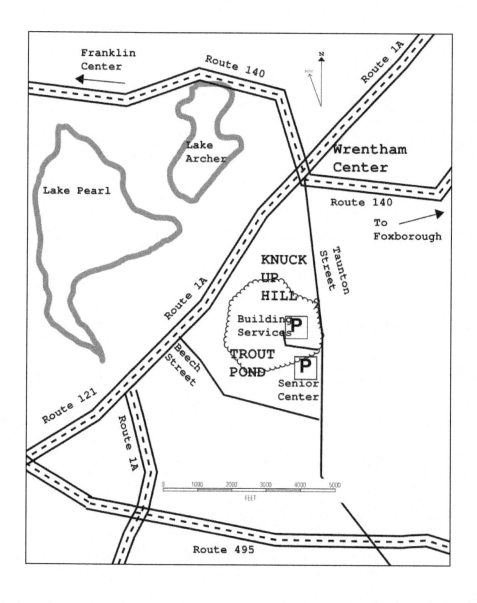

Trout Pond

Features: A loop trail along unimproved dirt track around ponds, stone walls, an old spillway, with varied terrain. Additional unimproved wide dirt trails through woodland.

WRENTHAM

Trail Map: Search "Wrentham Conservation Land," then download a pdf that contains maps of multiple conservation properties in Wrentham.

GPS Coordinates: 42°03'13.16"N 71°19'45.51"W

Directions: 400 Taunton Street, Wrentham.

From Wrentham Center: Rt. 140, cross the town common to Taunton St. Travel south about 1 mile past a school complex, and then look for the Wrentham Senior Center on the right. Park at the senior center, or follow the Building Services access road, next to the senior center, to the base of Knuckup Hill. Pond is on the left.

From Rt. 495: take Exit 15 (1A) north for 0.75 mile to the intersection with Rt. 121. Continue north on 1A for 0.3 mile, look for Beach St. on the right. Follow Beach St. 1 mile to the T with Taunton St., and turn left. Wrentham Senior Center is on the left about 0.3 mile farther on Taunton St. Park at the senior center, or continue past the senior center to the access road on the north side of the senior center, take the fork to the right toward the Building Services offices 0.2 mile, and park on the side of the road. The pond is on the left.

Cost: None.

Bathrooms: At the senior center when open.

Best Time to Visit: Year-round.

Trail Conditions: Unimproved dirt track, graded, wide paths.

Distance: 0.5 mile.

WRENTHAM

Parking: At Wrentham Senior Center, or just past the senior center at the Building Services Department. Park along the road, within view of Trout Pond.

Take the paved Building Services Department road that branches off to the right of the senior center, then park on the side of the road within sight of Trout Pond for a quick stroll. It is possible to walk around the entire pond (actually two small ponds with a walkway between them). The small dam that created the pond has an interesting spillway built of stone.

On the far side of Trout Pond the trail continues through woodland, with views of stone walls, a stream, and various plants. It's an easy walk that stops at Beach St.

Trout Pond and Knuckup Hill are in such close proximity that for some nice variety, combine the two walks into a single outing.

Woonsocket, RI

WOONSOCKET

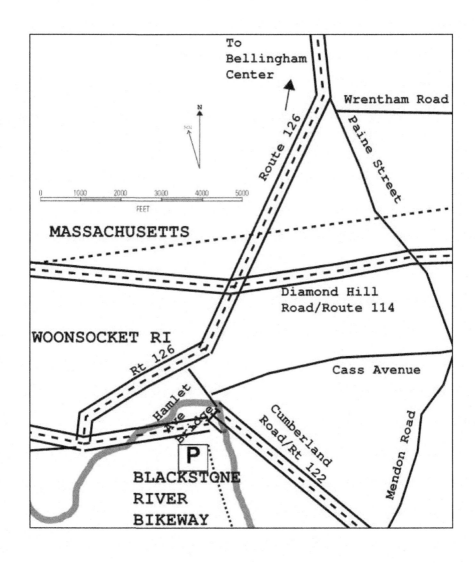

WOONSOCKET

Blackstone River Bikeway

Features: Handicapped-accessible paved rail-trail, river views, waterfalls, remnants of the Blackstone River Canal.

Trail Map: Search "Cycle Blackstone River Map" then click on Blackstone River Bikeway.

GPS Coordinates: 42°0'8.27"N 71°29'55.34"W

WOONSOCKET

Directions: **From Rt. 146 north:** take Rt. 99 for 2.7 miles to Rt. 122, (end of Rt. 99, Woonsocket), then turn left onto Rt. 122 Cumberland St. Travel 1.3 miles to the light at Hamlet Ave. Bridge. Turn left at the light, cross the bridge, take an immediate left at the next light. Look for "River's Edge Recreational Complex" sign on the left.

From Bellingham: take Rt. 495, exit 18, Rt. 126 south (S. Main St.) 2 miles, cross Rt. 140 at Bellingham center. Continue on Rt. 126 for 3.8 miles to Pulaski Blvd., bearing right and staying on Rt. 126, past the Stop & Shop Plaza and bearing right to stay on Rt. 126 into Rhode Island for 1.3 miles. At Social and Clinton Sts. (the Social Street Flatlands), bear right onto Social St. one block; take the first left onto Cumberland St., (it becomes Rt. 122), travel 0.5 mile, go past the Cass Ave. light. At the next light, turn right onto Hamlet Ave. and cross the Hamlet Ave. Bridge. Take the first left past the bridge, and the parking lot is immediately on the left. Look for a large blue sign saying "River's Edge Recreation Complex."

Cost: None.

Bathrooms: At the snack bar near the trailhead in Woonsocket when open; and at Kelley Museum, Cumberland-Lincoln line, when open.

Best Time to Visit: Year-round.

Trail Conditions: Paved rail-trail, few grade crossings.

Distance: 14 miles from Woonsocket south to Central Falls, RI.

WOONSOCKET

<u>Parking</u>: Paved parking for 25 cars, and additional packed gravel parking next to the soccer fields. For additional parking locations in RI, search "Blackstone River bikeway path," and scroll down for parking.

A real pleasure for cyclists and walkers, the 14 miles of paved bike trail along the Blackstone River Bikeway involve few grade crossings. The bikeway, part of the Blackstone River Valley National Historic Park, ties into the River's Edge Recreation Complex in Woonsocket, with parking adjacent to the Hamlet Ave. Bridge, Woonsocket. Additional parking areas are available south into Cumberland, following Rt. 122, and in Lincoln, RI. In the fall of 2016, an additional portion of the bikeway is slated to open in Blackstone (see Blackstone section of *Easy Walks*).

In winter, the gates to the Woonsocket recreation complex are closed, but walkers as well as skiers are welcome. Beware of packed-down icy areas.

The Blackstone River flows directly next to the Woonsocket-owned recreation area, which offers a small playground, modest putting greens, soccer fields, a building with a snack bar, restrooms in season, plus additional parking adjacent to the putting greens.

Along many parts of this Rhode Island portion of the rail-trail the river is in sight. Cormorants, geese, and mallards populate the river, while migrating waterfowl visit in spring and fall. Look for muskrats, osprey, great blue herons, mergansers, cedar waxwings,

WOONSOCKET

and bluebirds. The bikeway is paved, often shady, with benches, pull-off spots, and views of the river and waterfalls along its length.

Resources

Websites come and go. Look for additional information by searching for the websites of the organizations that oversee properties in this area. Suggested organizations include the following:

- Blackstone River Valley National Heritage Corridor
- Blackstone River Valley National Historic Park
- Massachusetts Audubon Society
- Friends of the Upper Charles
- Friends of Upton State Forest
- Friends of the SNETT
- Grafton Land Trust
- Metacomet Land Trust
- The Trustees of Reservations
- U.S. Army Corps of Engineers
- Friends of Hopedale Parklands
- Warner Trail

You may also find information about area trails by searching these topics: state recreation sites, Department of Conservation and Recreation (DCR) in Massachusetts. Check town websites, and look under "Conservation Department." Several area towns have started hiking clubs; search by town to see if there is a hiking club nearby.

Look for town forests in specific towns. Some towns have extensive information about their open spaces.

Local Cemeteries

In addition to the trails listed in this book, consider your local cemeteries as destinations to explore. Many are paved, birds love these areas, and the neighbors are quiet!

The biggest challenge when visiting cemeteries is parking—many have little parking, so take care to look for signs, and educate yourself about the rules for visiting your area's cemeteries, including policies about stone rubbings or picture-taking, to learn the hours when visitors are welcome. Above all, keep in mind that these are places set aside for remembrance, so be respectful while visiting.

Author's Note

Thank you for reading this book. I'm always thrilled to learn that readers have been able to use the information I've worked so hard to share. It's even nicer for me when I hear that this publication has encouraged families to get outside to spend time together in the outdoors.

Take a minute to write a review

If you found this book to be useful, please take the time to tell others about it. A review posted on Amazon is a real gift, whether you loved the book or have a criticism.

Here's a little about me

A native Floridian, I came to New England for college—and snow. I stayed after college, and have never tired of the rocks, ponds, hills, streams, (and the snow!) in this area of Massachusetts. How lucky I am to be able to write about the places I love.

As a personal and family historian, I search for and then listen to the stories of people's lives. Sometimes I hear these stories in a person's living room, and walking local trails I "hear" the stories of an area, "seeing" those who lived long before me.

My favorite stories are those that reveal otherwise untold events in a person's life. Exploring new trails, I try to work out the hidden stories of the landscape. Stone foundations appear in now dense woodland, a reminder that a family (or families) once made a home in what is now a quiet spot in the forest. Many of the trails we walk were once cart paths that brought goods from farms to towns over muddy, rocky, rutted tracks. These untold stories keep me coming back, observing, wondering, and learning.

Keep in touch

If you're on Facebook, come on over and "like" *Easy Walks in Massachusetts*. Learn where I'm traveling to next, get a peek at updates to these books as well as places that will be included in future publications. Let me know what you're up to in the out-of-doors. You can always get in touch at www.marjorieturner.com, or by email at Marjorie@marjorieturner.com